BUSINESS©
DOCTORS
ACHIEVE YOUR VISION

D1635555

BREAKING BIG

THE BUSINESS DOCTORS' NO-NONSENSE GUIDE TO ACHIEVING BREAKTHROUGH GROWTH FOR YOUR BUSINESS

CAPSTONE
A Wiley Brand

Registered office

John Wiley and Sons Ltd, The Atrium, Southern Gate, Chichester, West Sussex, PO19 8SQ, United Kingdom

For details of our global editorial offices, for customer services and for information about how to apply for permission to reuse the copyright material in this book please see our website at www.wiley.com.

Library of Congress Cataloging-in-Publication Data

Levington, Matthew, 1965–

  Breaking big : the business doctors' no-nonsense guide to achieving breakthrough growth for your business Matthew Levington, Rod Davies.

      pages cm

  ISBN 978-0-85708-393-7 (paperback)

    1. Small business–Growth. 2. Strategic planning. 3. Small business marketing. I. Davies, Rod, 1957– II. Title.

  HD62.7.L48 2014

  658.4'01–dc23

                                    2014011440

A catalogue record for this book is available from the British Library.

ISBN 978-0-857-08393-7 (pbk)

ISBN 978-0-857-08412-5 (ebk)   ISBN 978-0-857-08411-8 (ebk)

Cover design by Dan Jubb

Set in 11/14.5 pt Gill Sans Std by Toppan Best-set Premedia Limited

Printed in Great Britain by TJ International Ltd, Padstow, Cornwall, UK

Contents

BUSINESS ©

DOCTORS

A C H I E V E   Y O U R   V I S I O N

Business Doctors is a business support franchise, dedicated to helping small- and medium-sized businesses achieve their vision.

We are a network of experienced business people, passionate about sharing our skills and experiences.

Our aim is to offer 'hands-on' support to business owners, enabling them to overcome their individual challenges and helping them to achieve their aspirations for growth.

Whilst we operate within the consulting industry we are not traditional consultants. Our approach is different and involves getting into the nuts and bolts of businesses providing practical advice every step of the way.

Business Doctors has developed and helped transform hundreds of companies across a spectrum of industries, filling a gap in the market between the big four consultancies and specialist individuals.

The strength of the Business Doctor brand, combined with our holistic approach and alignment to government-funded support programmes, has helped us to become the fastest growing business support network in the UK.

We don't just coach – we get on the pitch!

The business was founded in 2004 by Matthew Levington and Rod Davies. They have built a national network of Business Doctors across the UK and are rapidly becoming recognized as the preeminent business support brand/service serving the nation's 4.8 million SMEs.

Matthew Levington

Intelligent, talented individuals who enjoy fast-paced, challenging environments make ideal business consultants and advisors. Matthew certainly fits the bill. A veteran of the highly-competitive and rapidly-evolving media industry, Matthew started his career in sponsorship and promotions at Piccadilly Radio. He quickly moved up the corporate ladder at EMAP, and was soon displaying his talents in a series of senior roles.

Matthew became Managing Director of Crash FM in Liverpool after its failed launch, and managed to reverse its fortunes by attracting the valuable (and fickle) youth market and the advertising revenues that follow. Matthew moved to Chrysalis stations Galaxy 105 in Yorkshire, followed by Galaxy 102 in Manchester, one of the UK's largest radio markets.

Matthew revived the underperforming Manchester station with bold, carefully calculated strokes that included the appointment of a senior management team, relocation to the city centre, and a determined focus on building a profile amongst the city's advertisers, businesses and communities.

Matthew's relevant business experience and talent for turn-around led him to found Business Doctors Ltd. with Rod. This unique opportunity to promulgate his hands-on style and to have a major impact on clients' bottom lines made Business Doctors the ideal venue for Matthew's many competencies and talents.

Rod Davies

The Management Consultancies Association (MCA) defines management consultancy as the application of knowledge, techniques and assets to improve organizational performance and implement business solutions. With extensive expertise, diverse experience, and a mastery of proven marketing and organizational strategies, Rod Davies has the profile of a premiere management consultant.

He has spent more than 25 years at the executive level of high-profile chemical, packaging, paper, stationery, textile and property businesses. He ran a successful paper merchant business in the Arabian Gulf. Rod was instrumental in turning around almost a dozen companies, from a £6m carpet manu-facturer to a £100m division of one of the largest global integrated paper producers.

While he has proved himself exceptionally capable of helping companies to improve their performance, Rod's personal approach and taste for getting his hands dirty makes him so much more than a consultant. Rod rolls up his sleeves and collaborates closely with owners, directors and managers, seeing to it that they get the tools and knowledge they need to succeed, both personally and professionally.

This zealous drive to advise and empower led him to form Business Doctors Ltd. with his business partner, Matthew Levington. Rod and Matthew have crafted a Strategic Planning and Advisory service with a unique emphasis on people-led change.

Acknowledgements

First and foremost we would very much like to thank all of our Business Doctors clients that we have worked with over the last 10 years, for giving us the direct insight, inspiration and very rewarding experiences that have motivated us to write this book.

All the examples, insights and shared knowledge featured in *Breaking Big* are drawn from the collective experiences of the Business Doctors Network – all of whom are accomplished business people in their own right. We are a 'consultancy speak' free zone so hopefully, you will appreciate that all of our thoughts and ideas are taken directly from the hands-on, front-line business experience.

No one individual (or business guru) has all the answers – at Business Doctors, we firmly believe that successful business is rooted in sharing experiences and knowledge without expectation of reward or return. Having said that we would like to acknowledge one particular person, Christian Annesley, who has helped us take a diverse collection of thoughts and ideas, and transform these into a coherent order of words that are hopefully easy to read and apply to your own business.

Christian Annesley supported Matt Levington and Rod Davies in producing *Breaking Big*. Christian is an experienced editor, writer and communicator. He began his career in journalism and these days spends most of his time helping businesses to tell better stories and reach out to the right audiences, whether online, in print or in person.

Introduction: It's all about YOU!

Running a business is often exciting but rarely easy.

If you are a business leader, you know that every day there are important decisions to be made and opportunities to be explored that make the best of your people and your company's commercial prospects. Those who are capable of making the right calls, for the right reasons, will see their business thrive – and enjoy the ride.

So, for the business leaders out there, how can this book help? First of all, *Breaking Big* isn't just another book of dry business theory – the world has enough of those already. Yes, it contains plenty of helpful advice and clear thinking, but you'll soon see that the point of these pages is to motivate and inspire you to take the right decisions based on the best possible insights into YOUR business and its customers. As the title of this introduction suggests, you'll find that this is a book about YOU and what you need to find out – about yourself and about your business – to achieve personal and commercial success.

Is there a formula we are about to thrust on you to guarantee success? Not a formula, no. To succeed you will have to go on a journey of discovery to work out what matters, and there are some tools that you might find useful to apply along the way. But this book has partly been written as an antidote to the usual business consultancy straitjacket: you know, the one which sees an 'expert' paid a small fortune to scrutinize the recent history of a company in order to produce a predictable report that identifies various points of failure that can be fixed – just fancy that! – if the consultant's specialist expertise is further applied.

This is YOUR business, these are YOUR opportunities

In *Breaking Big* we take a different approach. That's because there are far better ways to get to the truth of what a business needs – and all of them start by turning the focus back firmly on YOU, the leader in the hot seat. This belief and principle has always guided Business Doctors, the business-support organization that we first founded back in 2001 – and continue to develop and run today. Since those early days the basic premise of enabling structured self-reflection by business leaders, partly by asking the right questions, has been refined and tested by us in hundreds of different contexts. And guess what? It really works.

Don't worry, what you aren't about to get is page after page stuffed with self-help platitudes. The point we want to make – and the point that Business Doctors has always made – is that YOU know the issues your company faces better than anyone, and if you can only make the space and time to explore the challenge fully, with an open and positive mind, greater commercial success and personal fulfilment will follow.

Stop fire-fighting and get inspired again

Where does a journey like this start? It starts without pre-conceptions and with a blank page.

Most business leaders think they know their business, having immersed themselves in the minutiae of its day-to-day challenges for many years.

The trouble is, that's what's holding them back. Nearly all company directors spend their days (not to mention nights and weekends) dealing with immediate operational issues. It means there is rarely a moment to step away from all the noise and activity to take stock of what's happening in a more considered way: whether what they are doing day to day is working for the business; whether it is using their talents and know-how and relationships effectively; whether it is keeping them energized and happy.

These are big questions that should not be ignored. After all, companies are usually started by someone inspired by a dream or a big idea. Rediscovering that inspiration or dream can be challenging, but putting it off isn't an option for anyone serious about this book's message.

Inspiration takes many forms, of course, so be as challenging and creative as you want when it comes to working out what exciting looks like. The point is, we can all agree that it's only once you know what truly gets you excited that you can plan for more of the same. That's step one on the journey, and something that we'll explore fully in the book's early chapters.

Great vision, happy customers

By working out what makes you tick, you'll soon start working out what makes – or could make – your company great again. When did that ambition that you once had start to wane? Whether it was last month or last year, getting back your mojo and your self-belief is a wonderful antidote to the daily grind. As the love-him-or-loathe-him tycoon Donald Trump once said: 'If you're going to be thinking anyway, you might as well think big.'

Once a bold company vision starts to come together again, so will the strategy that's needed to make it a reality. And here's where a bit of data-crunching and analytics, allied to some structured, customer-focused thinking, will really help.

Why? Because any vision for success has to be based on reality and hard facts, rather than gut instinct. Entrepreneurs aren't always brilliant at the detail, preferring the grand plan and the big idea, so some outsourced rigour is what's called for here – and there are few clearer disciplines in business than the bottom line: love all your customers, by all means, but which ones make you money and which ones don't?

A clear-eyed analysis of the reality – of each customer, if necessary, and certainly each product line or service – should get you closer to the truth of your business vision and its prospects. What you find might be surprising or even shocking, but the effort will definitely pay its way. And it's what a large part of this book is about.

The customer is always right there

Some things are worth repeating. If there is one theme that *Breaking Big* returns to again and again it's the importance of the customer. Much of what follows pays the customer lots of attention – and then heaps even more on top.

We make no apology for this: a strong business needs to grow its sales to stay strong, and sales require customers that will buy and buy again. As we've already said, it's absolutely crucial that this quest for sales is aligned with your personal values and enthusiasms and the principles of the business, but equally it's fundamental that neither side of this equation suffers neglect:

1. Understand your vision and what makes you different and special.
2. Know what your customer is buying and why.

Love your staff

Our final word of preamble, before we leave you to dive in, is about the importance of managing and supporting the best people you can find the business. It sounds obvious, but plenty neglect this and suffer the consequences.

Business is a team game, but companies rarely grow logically, because needs change all the time. This means it's imperative to keep a close eye on who is doing what in a company, and to ask yourself as often as necessary what else they might be better off doing (that includes you, by the way).

There is plenty more to this, and plenty to be done. We'll explore it fully in the book's penultimate chapter. Whatever you do, however, the basic message is this: you should do everything you can at all times to ensure your staff never feel like passengers. An unhappy member of staff is soon an ex-member of staff, which usually benefits no one.

By the way, the chapters that follow are best read in sequence and in one go, but *Breaking Big* can be treated as a reference book too. Dip in and out of any section or chapter and the advice will still hold true. What you really mustn't do, however, is leave this book on the shelf gathering dust, like an expensive consultant's report you should never have commissioned in the first place. Read it, act on it, and feel the benefit!

Part One

THE RIGHT START

Every journey needs a beginning. This is where yours starts.

Chapter 1

Time to ditch the business plan?

Sometimes it's hard running a business. Where are all the good people to be found? When you do find them, why are they so expensive? Who to trust? Why aren't we making any money again this month? How on earth have we just lost that key customer?

It might be understandable to feel bogged down from time to time as the obligations and issues pile up, but a successful business needs a real plan. That's what this book is about.

Question: when is a plan not a plan? Answer: when it's a business plan.

Don't worry, no more riddles of any sort, we promise. But every business has stories to tell and many of these stories find their way into – or are created for – business plans of one sort or another. But are they really plans that are actively used and followed? Very rarely.

Just stop to think for a minute. If your company has been around for even a few years, you are sure to have such plans sitting on your company's servers somewhere:

- **A business plan** you wrote in order to raise some bank money, complete with sales projections and growth plans that you've not necessarily looked at since.

- **A financial plan** you created to pitch to serious would-be investors somewhere along the way. Likely this plan is something you've looked at and acted on in small ways since, for all the detailed financial modelling that was included, and the careful business case that was made at the time to present a really investable company.

Be honest, though: neither these plans nor any others that you've created are live working documents, are they? They are written looking forwards, maybe, but most – or all – were created to fulfil a particular need at a particular moment in time, and their usefulness doesn't usually extend very far beyond that.

There are other ways to think about your plans though, and it's the creation of and commitment to a different sort of plan – a genuinely strategic, lived and acted-upon plan – that is at the heart of our thinking.

Now, we know that talk of strategy makes plenty of business leaders wary. After all, the world is full of high-charging management consultants who like to talk about 'strategy' a lot – and then send through a prettily produced document and bill.

But strategy does matter – and it mustn't be allowed to become a dirty word in business. In fact, it matters so much it's worth saying what it means: one useful definition describes it as the effort to align external opportunity with internal capability. And you should add to this our belief that the right kind of strategy is also something for a business and its leaders to follow and swear by, so it becomes nothing less than a living, breathing inspirational framework that guides day-to-day activities and behaviours.

Get inspired

Is that too high-minded for you? For some it might be. But we think it's time you put aside any world-weariness or cynicism and started to look for ways to get inspired again – for your sake and the sake of your company.

Without doubt many owners of smaller businesses think that strategy sounds like something that's nice in theory but a bit corporate – and a bit irrelevant to the daily juggling and distractions of the reality of keeping the lights on and the show on the road.

But it's a fact that every company, large or small, needs a proper strategic plan in order to grow and evolve. If you accept this point – and you are reading this book, so we reckon you do – the next question is the biggie: how do you get there?

That's what the book you are holding is all about. If this is our scene-setting chapter, those that follow take a step-by-step approach to the challenges of building and growing a business to achieve a vision that manages to align the personal aspirations of the leadership of a business with the real-world, day-in and day-out plan for that business.

Where exactly does inspiration or passion fit in? Right at the beginning no less: we think it's the starting point for everything. Companies are started by passion and belief. The point about creating a new strategy for the business as it looks now – however many years in you are – is to reignite that passion and belief for the business and where it is headed, and apply it in a structured way every day.

Harnessing all that know-how and enthusiasm anew is not something that's achievable in one giant, transformative leap. But by making lots and lots of small changes in many areas you will soon find you are in fact doing something big anyway. Once the journey is embarked on, with real enthusiasm and passion for where things are headed, you might be surprised how quickly positive change follows.

Clarity not complication

Here's a statement for you: many businesses start out relatively simple and get more complicated – and more challenging to run.

Fair enough – or not?

Sure, when you are busy juggling the priorities of business, things can FEEL complicated, but that's not the same thing as true complexity.

Business is usually pretty simple – and when it starts to feel like there is too much happening and things are out of control then it's time to make things simple again.

How? By getting on with creating that real-world strategy that starts with your passions and looks in detail at the business from all sides – at its strengths and weaknesses, at its products or services, at its customers and their needs, at its people, at the competition out in the marketplace, at your aspirations as a leader, and so on.

The purpose of this sort of analysis is not just to create an up-to-date list of headline points but to start drilling down into the detail and then to take some big calls on how things need to be – and to make the necessary changes.

We'll look at the nuts and bolts of this approach in the chapters ahead, but first here's another way to look at the opportunity you need to take.

No death by chocolate

Imagine you own a chocolate business. In the early days life is sweet. You bring out three luxury chocolate products and start selling them through a network of high-end gift and chocolate retailers.

Buoyed by your early success you later invest in selling direct – through a dedicated ecommerce website and through a network of retail outlets you establish across the UK. You also branch out from your luxury chocolate range into some middle-market and mass-market products, eyeing the prospect of supermarket sales and more.

But as the company grows and the opportunities keep popping up, you find that the challenges multiply too. Cocoa prices and the cost of other raw ingredients keep on rising, squeezing margins, while the complexities of producing dozens of confectionary products from a single manufacturing site for a growing number of customers with different expectations and cultures, and of overseeing dozens of retail branches across the country, with all of the staffing and property-related challenges that go with that, starts to take its toll. There is competition now coming from all directions, too, as others have moved in on the market niche you first identified and have undercut you on price. Suddenly things are not so rosy.

What to do? While most might just carry on working with the logic of the business that's been created, distracted by cash flow and staff and customers and all of those other things it is hard to plan for in business, really what's needed is a root-and-branch rethink.

Perhaps some data-crunching shows that nearly half of revenues are coming from just 4 products out of 24, or that web profits are sharply rising while the majority of the company's retail outlets are barely in the black. Or maybe it's the factory that needs to go as the economics of outsourcing manufacture to more sophisticated and efficient production facilities elsewhere make perfect sense. Or perhaps much of the value in the business really lies in the strength of its brand name and certain products and what's needed is a marketing campaign that makes the most of that feel-good brand to drive mass-market sales.

Whatever the challenges that are identified, and whatever the strategy that's ultimately adopted, the other point is that any change that's brought in has to be applied with clarity right across the business. Senior directors, middle managers, those running the retail operations, the marketing team, the accounts department, those on the floor in the factory – lasting change will only come if everyone understands the ultimate objective and the part they are playing in its delivery. Getting people involved creates accountability but fosters commitment too, particularly if individuals are being given real ownership and responsibility for their contribution. It's a theme we will explore in detail later in the book and it goes to the heart of creating a truly successful strategy.

Make your strategy come alive!

Getting started with any strategy can often feel overwhelming. What's the best first step to take? What questions should you be asking yourself and the rest of the board?

If this fills you with any kind of dread, we've good news: in our experience the main resource you need to get things moving in the right direction is **TIME** – just enough of it to set aside all the operational issues so you can stop and think.

Start with a day

How long will it take? Well, a committed day is a great first step. When was the last time that all the company's stakeholders came together for a whole day to look at the medium- to long-term plans for the business? In all likelihood it was a while ago or has never even happened. Even if it is something that does happen on occasion, are such 'away days' really focused on strategy or do they see everyone involved talking shop and getting mired in operational issues?

One way to ensure that a day of talk isn't time wasted is to bring in an outsider to facilitate it and make sure it stays on track. Just as non-executive directors can bring fresh perspectives to some boardrooms, having someone at a strategy away day who is detached and focused on the objectives of the day could prove the difference between more chat and real strategic change.

A facilitator like this doesn't have to be an expert on your particular business and market either. In some ways involving someone who isn't an industry insider, with no particular understanding of the market or sector, works best. You just need someone with a good business brain, an objective view on the issues being raised, and a willingness to stick to the day's agenda.

What else will make the day work well? It needs to involve only the really key decision-makers, for starters. Some of those you ask to come might not be thrilled at the idea of taking time out like this, with operational issues to worry about, but if they are true decision-makers for the business they need to be there and put aside any reservations.

You also need to be clear about the agenda and how things are going to work. If you want to start work on a plan that will build the business over the next three to five years, say, everyone who's coming should understand that and realize that immediate operational issues won't be covered. Some might baulk at that suggestion, but it's important to remember that day one of even a five-year plan is the next working day. This isn't just blue-sky thinking but a chance to take important calls that will have an immediate impact.

Structuring the day

OK, so you've got everyone's buy-in and the day is in the company calendar. How can you maximize the chances of it being useful and even transformative for your business?

Step one is to set aside all the 'now' chatter, maybe by emphasizing ahead of the meeting just what's up for discussion – and what isn't. Change causes disruption and won't be embraced by everyone, particularly in a company where profits are being made and there are reasons to see the company as a success. Equally if a company is not doing so well the dynamic can be awkward too: some won't feel comfortable confronting things, frightened of what they may find out. Perhaps a company was strong once but is now in decline – if so, it's not an easy thing to face up to and some may prefer to treat the current predicament as 'a minor blip' and nothing more.

How you play things up front depends on your particular dynamic, but it's crucial to be explicit at every step. When Business Doctors gets involved in these kinds of days, the broad agenda often looks something like this:

1. Why are we even doing this? Understanding stakeholders' *personal* aspirations.
2. What's important to us? Core values and your business DNA.
3. What business are we in? (Clue: it's not what we sell but what our customers buy.)
4. What's the vision? What does *Breaking Big* look like for us?
5. Understanding the big picture and future proofing your business.
6. Market opportunities for growth.
7. GIVE analysis (Great, Improve, Vulnerable, Edge). Understanding our capabilities and what makes us different.
8. Strategy: defining a clear focus for growth.
9. Making it happen: critical success factors and an action plan.
10. What gets measured gets done.

That's a ten-point plan that should provide a solid basis for the day's activity – and those points also go the heart of the vision we've set out in this book. If you flick back to the contents page you'll see there's a close match between the chapter headings and the notional agenda for the strategy day that's such a first important step in making the necessary change.

What you might find out

No two company strategy days will be the same, of course, but many of the moments of realization and clarity that punctuate the day may look similar.

Starting at the top, that first point on the agenda – **shareholder aspirations** – is a big topic in its own right, and one we will cover in depth in Chapter 2. In the corporate world it might sound quite neutral, but for smaller, privately owned companies it's anything but. Really the question couldn't be any bigger. Why are we in business? Why are we doing this day in and day out? What do we all want personally from running and having a stake in this business?

It makes sense to start here because you can only begin to work on a strategy for the business once the personal aspirations are known: the two sides of the equation – the people and the business – really have to be aligned if a strategy is going to work.

And what kinds of issues come up? Well, for some it might prompt reflection on a work–life balance that has become skewed out of all recognition; for others it might lead to other kinds of soul-searching; for others still it might be the simplest thing in the world to articulate some business-related and personal aims and where the two intersect.

One thing we've noticed is how rarely business is primarily about the bottom line. In fact, plenty out there are happy to say these days that they simply want a profitable company that is growing and provides a liveable income. For others, the dream may be a little bigger in terms of financial rewards, and maybe a little simpler in terms of balancing priorities, but in most cases there will be some complications or tensions that need to be worked through and resolved.

The next two points on our list take us back to basics and are all about understanding the core values, goals and purpose of the business – why it was started, what it's purpose is now – as seen through the eyes of its directors and stakeholders. Here you sometimes get some extraordinary insights emerging once those involved start to open up and get to grips with what's being asked, not least when differences emerge between stakeholders over the values and trajectory of the business. Remember, often businesses are started because an individual or individuals did not share the values of their employers, so this is often a fundamental area to explore.

Beyond that point about values, the simple-sounding question of what the purpose of the business is can also generate surprising revelations and insights. For example, we once sat down with the directors of a company that billed and promoted itself primarily as a security firm. In the course of the session, however, it became clear that the real business of the company went far beyond security, into every aspect of the site services and local services support it offered to its customers (in the case of this company, usually construction companies working on building sites). Once the penny dropped, the MD was straight on the phone to the marketing agency that were poised to send the latest glossy company brochure to the printers. He called a halt to the print run because he now saw the story it delivered – with ranks of gleaming security vehicles lined up on the cover – was way off target.

The question of a company's vision and goals comes up under that **business vision: destination** heading and also under the next point on the strategy day checklist, **future-proofing**. The first exercise, about visionary goals, is a chance for everyone to get excited and think about where the company might end up in an ideal world – how big it might become and what new opportunities it might grab if everything worked out perfectly. This can be quite cathartic, just giving all involved the permission to put aside mundane realities for a moment and share their dreams. Some of it might not even turn out to be all that far-fetched or unrealistic, which is when things can get seriously exciting.

By contrast **future-proofing** is grounded more firmly in reality and the known. This is a chance for a step-by-step walkthrough of the social, economic, technological and political factors that could potentially impact on the business. And of course it's still a chance to ask some important questions and swap insights. Are there any opportunities or threats we need to explore together? What do they look like? How speculative or tangible are they? How do we progress the opportunities and avoid the threats? Clearly there's plenty of potential for something really important and exciting to come out of this part of the day, too.

Next up on the list – the part of the day we like to call **your market**, moving into the related area of **opportunities for growth** – is in many ways similar, in that it's a discussion grounded in the here and now of the business and in the known and the knowable. What does the current products-and-services mix in the business look like? What financial value attaches to each market opportunity? Who are our top ten customers and what do we know of their needs? Who are our suppliers and strategic partners? Are they the right ones and are we getting out of them what we should?

There's the potential for some genuine revelations to emerge from this part of the day, partly because it can often serve to highlight issues such as contradictions between the public face of the company and what it's known for, and some of the financial realities that often lie buried under the surface. Over and over again we see companies whose reputation has been built on a product or service that is no longer profitable, for example. One case that illustrates this nicely is a law firm we sat down with that had a huge reputation in criminal law but actually made its profits from personal injury cases. In fact, the criminal side of the firm was actually loss-making and being propped up by the profits coming through from personal injury work. It's a binary sort of example and demonstrates perfectly the kinds of tensions that crop up – but also the clarity that can emerge about what needs to happen next.

The top ten customers question is another from this section of the strategy day that is liable to get minds racing once explored. Experienced though we are at teasing these things out, for us it's still quite startling the extent to which companies fail to make the most of their customer base. The nascent potential just sits there untapped, year after year, with a circumscribed, transactional, often passive relationship that never gets moved on. But the potential to sell more and do more with your leading customers can be extraordinary.

An example, this time from a design agency we worked with that had a contract for the packaging designs for a major chocolate manufacturer. It was a nice slice of work from a company that was a lot bigger than many of the agency's other clients, and the directors were very proud of holding the contract. But it didn't take much effort to find out that only a small fraction of the chocolate company's total design spend – less than a fifth of its overall design budget – was going on packaging design. There was spend going into web design, point-of-sale, supplier brochures, you name it. But the agency had never ever tried to pitch for any of that work: it had just stuck with what it had. When it did ask, it was immediately right in the mix and started to win other pieces in the pie too – all because it asked and got the ball rolling. If you look at it from the customer's perspective, having six or eight or ten different design agencies on the slate was probably less appealing than having two or three really trusted agencies doing all the work between them – and wanting desperately to deliver in order to keep it that way.

There are lots of examples we could give to show the value of talking to customers and trying to meet their needs, but one of the best that's worth retelling now was the time that our strategy day reached the point where we started talking about the need to ask customers for meetings to find out their needs. It drew an instant negative response from one company director, who insisted his customers wouldn't be interested. So we challenged him on the spot: call one of them now and ask. He picked up the phone, put the question (this was his key customer, remember) and was amazed when the company instantly and delightedly accepted his invitation of an agenda-less meeting to get to understand each other better.

The **your market** section of the day covers much more than customers, of course – it might be your sourcing strategies and costs that come under the spotlight, say. Equally the **opportunities for growth** follow-up could head off in myriad directions. For now, though, let's move on. GIVE analysis is next on the list – and it needs a little explaining.

GIVE is an acronym that comes from these headings: Great, Improve, Vulnerable, Edge. In essence, it's a chance to be analytical and take a long, hard look in the mirror. Do we as a company understand our capabilities? What are we great at? Where can we improve? How and why are we vulnerable? What's our edge on the competition? What makes us different? Are we really distinct or is some of what we do or offer pretty forgettable and ordinary?

It's a crop of important questions that all aim to get to the root of what makes the company offer distinct and special. If a company has aspirations to take business away from others and to grow beyond the market through innovation it needs an advantage. What is that advantage, then? For smaller businesses it's unlikely to be based on cost as being cheap by doing things at scale is what many corporates are good at. What is the value being added, then? Why is what the company sells worth paying something extra for? The point here is that there will be things that make you uniquely attractive to your customers for various reasons – **BUT YOU REALLY NEED TO KNOW WHAT THOSE POINTS OF ATTRACTIVENESS ARE!**

Put it this way: many companies shout about the wrong stuff or go after the wrong customers – and often make both mistakes because the two things are connected. So this part of the day is an attempt to avoid that trap: to focus on what makes the company different or better; to sell to the right clients, rather than being scattergun; to get strategic. It should be a moment of clarity and insight.

The final three points on the ten-point list for the day will often take a lead from that GIVE analysis and what has already gone before, as the headings suggest: **strategy**, **making it happen** and **what gets measured gets done**.

If **strategy** sets out the beginnings of a way ahead in broad terms, the question of implementation – **making it happen** – is a first try at identifying the elements that will be needed to deliver, with **measurement** at the heart of things.

It starts with the people and with the suitability or otherwise of the current management and reporting structures. It will usually also look in detail at things like sales opportunities and strategies and at performance indicators for individuals and for the business. There will be a lot of work to do here beyond the big picture stuff, and much of it will have to wait for another day, but it's still possible to make headway and get some real clarity of purpose. It's amazing how often, when companies reach a certain size but haven't evolved a top-level management structure to manage them, the same needs end up being identified – someone to take on the role of managing director, someone else to become operations director, someone to take charge of finance, and a sales and marketing head too. There will be many variations on this pattern, but for a surprising number this kind of starting point gets things moving.

So there you have it: the whistle-stop tour of where we will take you over the rest of the book. From here onwards, we'll be rolling up our sleeves and getting down to some of the detail.

Chapter 2

It's the NOW show!

Business owners are busy people – we all know that. But some are actually too busy for their own good. That's because they – and maybe we're talking about **YOU** – are too busy to stop for a moment and step back from all the stuff that's filling up the day to ask themselves a really big question.

Why are you doing this?

We're sure that you **THINK** you know the answer to this one, but does what you would say off the cuff really answer the question? The **WHY** that's being asked here has nothing to do with keeping up with all your work obligations – the logic and demands of the business that's developed – and everything to do with your **UNIQUELY PERSONAL** needs and motivations. That's probably a different kind of **WHY** altogether from the one you were looking to answer.

How does today feel?

Companies are set up for all sorts of reasons. Some are established by restless serial entrepreneurs who spend their lives spotting opportunities and going after the best of them. Others are set up by someone following a vocation who is motivated to pursue that vocation as a business – perhaps because the prospects for doing so are better than the prospect of working for others for years to come. Others still are best called accidental entrepreneurs: those who aren't naturally entrepreneurial but who have been forced by circumstance to pursue opportunities on a self-employed basis – maybe because of redundancy – and over time have forged a business.

Despite the differences in these scenarios and mindsets, there's a good chance that all of these different sorts of entrepreneur will have been excited by creating a successful business and by its development at various moments along the way. But what about right now? Is the excitement and the passion still there? Or does work frequently become a stressful obligation and a chore? If so, what is the precise cause of that stress?

The point here is not to dwell on the negative side of what work means, but to encourage a rounded appraisal of your current situation that's honest and thoughtful. What's good about running and owning the business? Where would you like the business to head from here and have you got a plan to get there? What's challenging or stressful about the current state of play? What would you like to change if you could?

The finances of the business will likely play a part in some of this. Is the business making profits? Are those profits growing or shrinking? And if the company isn't making meaningful money, what are the prospects for turning the situation around?

Equally, finances are rarely the whole story. There are plenty of business owners out there who want a successful business that makes more and more money, but there are also businesses that provide a way of life for an owner that makes them feel fulfilled and provides a solid living – and the main objective is to maintain that happy situation for many years to come.

How (and what) to share

There's another aspect that we've left out so far – and this is where things can get complicated.

When it comes to thinking about the **WHY** of being in business, there's more than just you, the owner, to think about. Nearly every business of any size has more than one shareholder and probably has a board of directors, some or all of whom will have a stake. So what does the **WHY** look like for all of the various stakeholders in the business – and are they all in a position to be totally open with one another?

Openness, honesty and transparency are excellent principles, of course, but some situations won't be clear-cut. For some owners, the aspiration to prepare a business for a possible sale may simply be something that's too loaded an idea to put to the other stakeholders out of the blue. Instead, it might be necessary to initiate a more controlled discussion that goes only as far as the owner is comfortable and no further, in order to begin to lay the groundwork for broaching a bigger idea later on.

And remember, even when there is no particular issue in the mix that puts some things off-limits for now, a discussion between shareholders about aspirations will rarely be easy. For an individual owner to be frank and honest with himself or herself about such big, important ideas is usually difficult enough. Getting others to go through the same brutally honest appraisal of their personal situation and motivations, aspirations and worries in relation to the business – and then sharing that with everyone else involved – can be a hard step to take, particularly if no one is used to this kind of openness.

Also, what if the aspiration sharing does happen – but it turns out that the goals of several of those involved are poles apart? Here we reckon a surprisingly simple rule applies: once aired, different aspirations can nearly always be reconciled and accommodated. We'll go into more depth on this shortly, but what is harder to reconcile is where individuals have different basic values in relation to a business. That's an area where things can soon run into difficulties.

What do we mean by values in this context? In short, the basic principles you stick to when doing business and engaging professionally in all contexts. It's what governs your relationship with staff, suppliers and partners of various sorts – and how you think about your customers, too. Here's an example that should help.

The perfectionist and the pragmatist

Business Doctors worked for an extended period with the owner of a company that specialized in fit-outs of hotels, bars and restaurants. The company had lots of very satisfied clients, in large part because the owner of the business was an absolute perfectionist. As such, the fit-out work by the company was of very high quality, with few or any snaggings for customers to worry about.

As the company developed, it needed some more process and procedure to run more effectively and profitably – and to systematically address issues like site safety and quality control procedures.

So the perfectionist owner brought in an outsider with an excellent background in project management from a sizeable construction business.

On paper, at least, the match looked excellent – but the reality was very different. The new recruit was certainly a big-hitter with an excellent track record, but his values were different from those of the owner. For him, business was about making money and being good enough: i.e. get away with as much as you can under the terms of a contract in order to maximize profits – and if necessary have legal battles along the way, around the margins of a job, rather than go overboard to satisfy the customer.

In many ways the attitudes the newcomer held were industry-typical behaviours and values – but they were clearly a world away from the values of the owner, whose go-the-extra-mile approach was at the heart of his organization's values.

Despite having advised against taking this person on beforehand, we wanted to see things work out and to be proved wrong for the owner's sake; unfortunately the relationship soon ran aground. Within six months the two had parted company, with the newcomer taking his experience – and his particular values – on to another context where his approach was far more likely to be embraced. All in all, it was an expensive and draining lesson for the owner to learn.

Finding the common ground

If that's a useful demonstration of the importance of shared values among the stakeholders in a business, the other thing we'd also say is that aspirations and motivations can usually be reconciled and accommodated. It's a big claim to make, so what do we mean by it?

Simply this: so long as the stakeholders share the same basic values about how to run the business, whether they want different things from it should be a secondary issue. It doesn't have to get in the way of reaching agreement about and sticking to a strategy – it's just a question of finding enough common ground to work with from the outset.

Maybe you're still sceptical: some situations are asking for trouble, surely? What if Director A wants to try to grow the business aggressively for a few years and to look at the issue of succession in order to make a potential exit more viable further down the line, while Director B favours a steady-as-she-goes approach that gives a nice respectable income and a good work–life balance for as far into the future as possible?

The two positions might sounds poles apart – they are, of course – but experience tells us that if there is mutual under-standing and respect on both sides and a shared respect for the business it shouldn't preclude a plan that works for both parties. Investment in growing parts of the business might need to be more selective than Director A would like ideally; Director B might need to push herself harder at times and embrace certain initiatives that Director A wants to run with and can prove will work. Equally there might be the basis for a discussion about the respective equity stakes of the two partners, and whether Director B might want to consider relinquishing or selling a portion to Director A. Both sides will probably also be able to agree about the need and basis for a succession strategy that finds and develops the next generation of leaders to run the business when the current owners have moved on.

What matters is that there are choices to be made, even in this example, that should be able to give the company a workable strategy that suits all stakeholders well into the future.

Motivation matters

There's another important dynamic that needs attention too, because it affects motivation and becomes harder to address if it isn't sorted out properly in the first place.

Not all directors are created equal, are they? Very often you'll have the founder or founders of the business taking the lead, while others who have come in subsequently might play more of a secondary or supporting role that leans on their particular area of expertise.

There's nothing that's too challenging about that situation but where things can and often do get sticky is where there are equity-holding directors in the mix who haven't invested in the business in return for their slice.

For any shareholding director, putting your own money into the company pot in return for that stake matters a lot. Time and again when working with owner-managers who have run into difficulties, we've found that the problem arises from having directors in the mix who haven't put enough on the line to care. It doesn't have to be all that much – £20k or even less, potentially, might well be enough – but it can't and shouldn't be nothing.

The buck stops here

Here's a life-lesson story to ponder.

Business Doctors was working with an engineering business that was starting to struggle. The downturn had hit the fortunes of the business and it was poised to record a full-year loss for the first time. The owner, who had a 60% holding in the business, was working long hours and having sleepless nights about the unfolding situation, but he also felt quite isolated. His two partners in the business, both with 20% stakes, were carrying on regardless, without too much obvious concern, and leaving for home at 5pm every day without fail.

Why the difference in attitudes and stress levels? Look no further than this: the owner had gifted both men the respective 20% stakes they held – and the personal guarantee on the borrowing with the bank was also solely with the owner.

How were these two directors exposed to the fortunes of the business? The upside was that if the business was successful it would give them an increasingly valuable stake, but that was it: there was no downside as such – no money on the line, no home at risk, nothing to worry about if things went wrong beyond the usual employee's concern of being out of a job if the company failed.

You can probably guess what we are going to say now: we strongly believe every stake held by a director in a business must count for something, for all the directors to run the company together, taking collective decisions that everyone buys into.

A personal journey too

We opened this chapter by talking about the importance of understanding the personal aspect of being in business. It has been focused on how some personal motivations and values will feed into and impact on the business strategy, but also on how some of the structures within the business will dictate the dynamics between stakeholders as they start to think about and share their personal needs with a strategic goal in mind.

What else is there to say about personal interests and how they might feed the business strategy? For now, only this: hold onto what matters to **YOU** at all times and make sure that finds reflection in the business and how it's run. Sure, there are various interests to balance here, but every director has to be at least comfortable and ideally should be really delighted with the context that's been created. Never lose sight of that – and if things stray off course then you should immediately revisit why and try to reset the business as quickly and collaboratively as possible.

The next chapter takes this further, so read on.

Chapter 3

What makes your company tick?

Many would-be business owners are moved to take the plunge and launch their own venture because of a strong desire to work in a company context and environment with just the right vibe and values – somewhere they and those around them are happy to go every day and set to work.

It may or may not be something you've dwelled on much, but we're willing to bet that this question of values has at least been there in the background, informing the kind of business you want to run (or be involved with) all the way through your career.

But if values are important they are also easily neglected.

Have you ever faced a Monday morning where an excellent, high-performing employee walks into your office and says she is ready to quit? Or noticed how several more junior staff are coming into the office late and then moaning loud and long about the day ahead?

The chances are something like this has happened to you at some point, particularly as small businesses so often rely on key employees wearing so many different hats while the business owner is also getting pulled in several directions. Very often, these problems have their roots in the company culture heading off course.

But what's to be done if the culture is wrong or the values seem to have gone missing somewhere along the line?

Get back to basics – get SELFISH!

One place to start is with this core idea: the values of a business start with the business owner. When companies are founded, it's the founder's vision that sets the tone and points the way ahead. ('What kind of business do I want to create? This kind of business!')

But as companies evolve, that original founder's vision is diluted. That's to be expected of course, as others become involved and a business grows, but the founding principles of any business do matter – and are well worth retrieving and refreshing.

So how should you start to get some of that original vision back? By being more selfish.

In this context, a dose of selfishness isn't negative, even if it might sound that way. Running a business as it grows always involves an awful lot of thinking about the needs of others: of employees, of suppliers, of customers. There's even a good chance that a business owner will have periods where they are working long hours, and paying skilled staff handsomely, while taking very little money out themselves.

A selfish exercise

Being selfish is another way of saying that you need to focus temporarily on your needs and desires in order to understand them better. It's not something that many do, because few of us like to be selfish — we all know we are part of a bigger picture.

The best place to start the exercise is by asking yourself some important questions — and capturing your answers:

- What is most important to YOU in your personal and work life?
- What VALUES are most important to you?
- What is it that YOU want from the business?
- What kind of business do YOU want to be running?
- What is the current 'DNA' of the business? What is its character and how or to what extent is it defined by YOU and your beliefs?
- Do you live the values you have identified as important and are those same values shaping and defining the business?

If you take it seriously and apply yourself (and you should, of course!), a set of questions that looks like this or similar should generate plenty of ideas and material for you to ponder. It might be the first time for a long time that you've thought about this stuff, which tells its own story.

Take some time out here to complete the exercise we've outlined in the box. Once you've done that you should then work at refining the best of what you've gathered in a structured way; very soon you will have a document that you will be ready to share with others, at least through discussion if thrusting some sheets of A4 under someone's nose seems too formal. These further discussions are likely to be with trusted friends and family initially and soon enough with other directors in the business. It's all part of a process that will lead you towards forging – or reforging – a stronger connection between your values and the company's values and culture.

Talk time

The point where you feel clarity about your values and the way you want to see them adopted in the business is the natural moment to start discussing values with other directors or senior management in the company. You will probably have a good feel for how your fellow directors view the world and the company itself, but it's still a big thing to share in this way and start working towards a collective vision. Our advice: don't take it lightly but equally don't be too heavy-handed. It should feel natural to talk these things through – and a positive step towards creating a better business culture and ultimately a stronger business.

One risk here is that the director-level values discussion might reveal some uncomfortable truths about the different values of stakeholders. In most cases, though, defining and refining the shared values you will want the business to adopt should be a productive and even exciting exercise, revealing some of the possibilities for the company in the future. Again, it could easily be the kind of process that's explored as part of a wider discussion day – or could be something that's tackled separately as a first step.

Once those values are defined, in any event, there is much that's positive that can start to happen. Sharing those values and ideals with the rest of the company in a constructive way should unlock a refreshed sense of purpose and belonging. It will draw the staff in and get them engaged with something that should add an extra dimension of purpose to their working lives, and could transform external relationships too. All in all, it's a really exciting idea.

A word of warning, though. If there is a more-than-awkward gap to be bridged between the current reality and the values vision you want to share with the rest of the company, be ready for a longer haul and a few challenges.

Room for improvement?

You might merely get the answer you want to hear when you ask employees directly if all is well. But how else can you work out if the culture is off course – or your leadership is lacking?

Signs might include:

1. **Defensive employees.** Whenever someone senior points out an area that needs improvement or a problem that needs a remedy, employees react badly. Any business where honest dialogue is rare isn't on the right track, because it means employees aren't feeling supported enough to function effectively.

2. **Unbalanced relationships.** Think about whether some lower-level employees have frequent contact with members of the senior team and a strong relationship, while others hang back and don't get much support – whether coaching, mentoring or encouragement – from managers and from colleagues.

3. **Fear of risk-taking.** If key staff are reluctant to introduce innovation, stop to consider why. If senior management have blamed employees for missteps in the past, that can knock confidence and make even the most confident of staff more risk-averse.

4. **Too positive.** You might think that positive feedback from employees demonstrates a lack of problems, but it isn't necessarily so. Staff may not complain because they sense that negative comments are unwelcome.

5. **Talented people, average performance.** Talented people want to deliver great results, not only for your business but also for their CVs. If your star employees are delivering average sales, productivity and profitability, they are probably not getting what they need from the business.

6. **Customer complaints.** Customer responses to your company reflect their treatment by employees, and particularly front-line staff. If there are lots of complaints then something is surely wrong in the business culture. Worse, you may lose some customers permanently if some complaints that seemed like isolated minor concerns turn out to be really serious. Are your employees being discouraged by the company's ineffectiveness?

7. **Issues come up again and again.** Are you hearing the same problems over and over at meetings? That's

probably because little or no effective action is being taken to sort them out.

8. **Families don't attend company parties.** Of course this assumes you invite them! But if employees come alone to get-togethers that have a wider invitation list, it may indicate that spouses have a negative view of the company.

More than a mission statement

There are lots of ways to embark on building the right business culture (see the close of the chapter for a list on the theme). But the first point to make is that driving values in a business is about a lot more than putting a company mission statement on the wall, on the website and in the new-starters pack for employees.

There is nothing wrong with a nice, punchy list of values that really means something, but it's also important that your values and your company culture are focused outwards and about much more than the company's interests.

Here's an example of values that have been identified and are, we hope, strived for in practice by one UK utility company, captured on its corporate social responsibility pages online:

Challenging
We strive for continuous improvement

Committed
We are passionate about customer service

Purposeful

Everything we do leads to better customer service and better delivery

Reliable

We do what we say

Supportive

We create an environment where people can voice their opinions

We're receptive to other people's views

We consider the consequences of what we do

It's a fine set of ideals to organize around, but what about the detail? Some of that's there too, on the same page of the website.

Who we are and what we stand for

We're a water and sewerage services business, delivering the highest quality water and recycling it safely back to the environment.

We provide an essential service to our domestic and business customers and our years of service and a forward-thinking approach ensures our standing as the water company of choice.

What we want to achieve

If customers had a choice, they would choose us.

How we'll get there

- We aim to provide the best-in-class water and sewerage service, to be profitable and sustainable, and to act in the long-term interests of the wider community by:

- Working closely with customers and stakeholders.
- Delivering services at a reasonable cost.
- Doing what we say.
- Developing the best team.
- Being innovative.
- Investing in the right tools to get the job done well.
- Educating and informing the public.
- Improving financial performance.
- Being efficient and completing projects on time.

We hope you can see how the detail matters – and how this follow-up statement-of-intent is good in itself but still just a beginning. How can the organization ensure that all of these values are ideals that are being lived by its workers each and every day? That's where the real challenge lies.

The mission or value statement, then, is a useful reminder to help individuals to stay on track, but for values to work they have to be lived by each individual because the values are being shared in every part of an organization – and are not just on the wall. For that to happen they cannot be one-dimensional, but must of course be adopted and promoted internally to help everyone involved to develop and internal-ize that living belief in the organization's principles.

We are not saying it is easy, but it really is achievable.

Good enough to eat

A major, listed utility company employing thousands clearly has the resource to have a fully-rounded corporate social responsibility agenda to put on its website, but implementing it will probably be an order of magnitude harder than in a small, privately-owned business.

What difference can transforming a company's internal culture really make, then? The story of one restaurant business we worked for really brings it to life.

The business was founded back in the early noughties, and the founder had the idea that the culture would always be welcoming so that customers went away with positive memories of every visit.

The trouble is, that ideal wasn't something the owner ever shared with his staff, and the culture of the business that evolved was quite different, with employees behaving inconsistently.

The uneasy founder called us in at this point and, working together, we developed a company purpose and set of values that was eventually ready for sharing. Lots of off-site staff training and sharing sessions followed, and the immediate and longer-term results were startling. Within months, the restaurants were busier than they had ever been – and employee turnover in this high-attrition industry slowed dramatically to less than a sixth of the industry average.

What made the difference with this push was probably the effort to involve customers in staff fun and silliness from time to time, which generated a lot of goodwill. And there was also the renewed efforts of the business to be active in the communities where the restaurants were well established. As well as being good for worker morale, it built brand awareness and attracted some community-focused customers too.

Lastly, staff wellness was part of the value set defined by the founder, and his introduction of some collective, fun exercise routines for staff, together with subsidized gym membership (and encouragement to attend) made all the difference too.

Let's give the founder the last word: 'Since then most of our growth has been via word of mouth. The staff feel loved and treat the customers well, and everything flows from there. It's been a wonderful journey so far and one I wished I'd carried off from the beginning.'

Some journeys are harder than others

Not every effort to work at company culture will go so well, of course. Here's another example that started off some-where else altogether but ended up putting the company's values under the spotlight.

A few years ago we worked with a footwear business that supplied bespoke commercial footwear to business clients all over the UK and in Europe as well. Our analysis and engage-ment with the company soon revealed that customer percep-tions of the company were not what they should be – and mainly because the company had a track record of letting its customers down in various ways, but particularly in respect of sizing.

The problem had its origins in the company's systems and processes, and in its culture too. There was, frankly, a gap between the company's public pronouncements about its integrity and its stated customer-first culture, and the reality:

the company didn't have the systems and resources in place to deliver right-size items all the time at short notice, despite that being in the terms of most of its contracts, so it would deliver the wrong size items initially and deal with any resulting problems as a follow up.

This self-interested, short-term approach, ignoring the needs of customers, was something that needed a culture shift as well as practical change. It needed the company to acknowledge that not enough attention was being paid to its systems and processes in order for it to deliver as required.

Equally, the company could have come clean and committed only to longer lead times, though the risk of lost business was substantial in the competitive market space. The final point is that the culture itself, which allowed this situation to prevail for not weeks or months but years, needed to change dramatically. Making commitments that you can't possibly keep will look a lot like fraud to many of us, and it's not a values system that stands up to much scrutiny.

What value are values?

If those two examples, from our own direct contacts, tell two distinct stories about the impact of values on an organization, there are plenty of other examples out there in the wider marketplace – and some interesting questions around how easy or hard it is for companies to sustain cultures when new owners arrive.

Here's an example to think about as you start to ponder the values journey you might want to embark on within your own business.

The company and its values: Innocent Drinks

Innocent Drinks, founded in 1999 by three former university friends and known for many years not just for its smoothies but for its creative, non-corporate, ethical business culture and its charitable giving, announced in 2009 that a minority stake in the business was being acquired by the US soft drinks giant The Coca-Cola Company, with the three founders retaining operational control. If that announcement left some customers unhappy, the ownership really shifted a year later, in April 2010, when Coca-Cola increased its stake in the company to 58% from 18%. And then in February 2013 Coca-Cola increased its stake to over 90%, leaving the three founders with just a small minority holding.

Innocent's founders, led by Richard Reed, always made a lot of Innocent's business mission and values in the years before Coke became involved, saying, among other pronouncements, that a business has to have a mission and provide people with 'a clear idea' of who and what you are as a business. 'You have to be really clear on why you exist – for Google this is to organize all the world's information and for Innocent Drinks it is to get healthy food to people,' says Reed.

Added to this, Reed has also talked a lot about the importance of Innocent's people, describing the business as just the sum of its people. He emphasizes bringing out the best in people, engaging them, motivating them, and developing them: 'The most important thing you do as a business leader is recruitment and you need to know what you are looking for.'

Staff engagement and company values have also been prominent at Innocent, with everybody getting a share in the business and a share in profits, as well as the option to buy more shares. Every Monday morning the whole team gets together and everybody gets one minute to say what they are doing and there are some collective exercises. There is also an employee of the month scheme and a scholarship to be bid for so people can fund their passions.

At the other end of the scale, Reed acknowledges it also means you will need to lose the people who don't work out: 'You cannot run a team when someone is not pulling their weight.'

And there is the ethics dimension: 'At heart we are an altruistic company: we want to leave things a bit better than we find them,' says Reed. A minimum of 10% of profits go to charity.

It all presents an interesting proposition in the context of this chapter on values and culture, while also begging the question – the other big question for many companies – about whether company values and company culture can be maintained through different ownerships. In Innocent's case the question seems particularly pertinent, with a big US corporation like Coca-Cola buying a relatively small privately owned UK business.

It's striking, too, because it's clear that part of what Coke was buying when it invested in Innocent was the company's brand values. And it's an important point: company values really are worth something in the marketplace. But is it sustainable for a brand and business like Innocent to exist in the context of such a large corporation and still stay true to its founding principles? This is much more than just idle speculation: it's something for you to be thinking about in the context of company values and cultures, since exits and ownership changes are a fact of life in business. Which bits of your company values, if any, might be non-negotiable in the event of a sale?

Values that are worth having

Looking beyond the Innocent–Coke deal, these days there seem, more than ever, to be corporations that are keen to buy smaller firms held in good regard as businesses and by consumers – and, as is clear, part of what they are buying into is the culture and the values. Think here about Cadbury's purchase of the organic and fair trade chocolate business Green & Black's (meaning G&B is now owned by Kraft, which bought Cadbury). Or the 2013 purchase by supermarket monolith Tesco of the family-friendly restaurant chain Giraffe, partly in a bid to reposition itself in the public imagination. Are these kinds of tie-ups doomed to end in tears – or can the values and the culture live on?

Back, though, to you: will your company's values and culture live on effectively if you can get things right now? We really think they can.

Nine steps to building the right culture

1. **Communicate your dream and ensure it is operable.** Company mission statements are too often narrow and too business oriented. (What does: 'Be a leader in customer satisfaction' actually mean?) Your dream and your company culture needs to be focused

outwards, towards a higher good that extends well beyond the company's financial interests.

2. **Be clear about what you stand for.** Your personal priorities, values and principles set the culture. The best way to be clear about them is to engage team members, customers, and suppliers. People follow what you do, not what you say.

3. **Shape your organization for what it needs to win.** This includes the specific work you must do, the capabilities you need to build for a competitive advantage, and the career path for team members to bring this to life.

4. **Get your team right.** If you didn't know already, you need to know where you need help and where you need helpers. For real help, you will always need to seek out individuals who are smarter than you in their expert area, while helpers with the right can-do attitude give you the critical mass you need to get more routine stuff down, though the management team will need to dictate the tasks and make all the decisions. Always be quick to handle hiring mistakes.

5. **Set standards high.** You tell people every day what meets your standards when you agree or disagree with recommendations from your team. If you believe in your team, you set high standards and stick to them. A good team will step up to the challenge.

6. **Keep on training.** This might require a different mindset for some, but every interaction every day is a potential training event. Training means coaching rather than criticizing, to improve the outcome next time. Constant training is engrained in great leaders and great companies.

7. **Do symbolic things that create some buzz.** Even if just once or twice a year, you should carry through some symbolic actions that are meaningful to the team and other stakeholders, as well as being fun and giving direction.

8. **Expect to win, and act accordingly.** Customers can usually sense how motivated a company's people are just from seeing the product and how it gets presented to them. Customers want to buy from a winner, so ensure no one ever says sorry about price or quality, and make sure you never shy away from an opportunity to delight a customer.

9. **Have a goal and live it.** If you don't know your ultimate goal, you will never get there. And if the company's workers don't know the ultimate goal of the business, they can't get there either.

Chapter 4

What business are you REALLY in?

I t's time to start thinking hard about your customers.

With good reason, the early chapters of the book have looked at the inner workings of the business, but clearly that's only one aspect of the overall challenge.

Every business needs to deliver for its customers, but it is easy to lose sight of who those customers are and what they want. That they are spending with you is no indicator in itself that you have things right.

There are big questions to ask yourself – and to answer carefully:

- What are those that you sell to buying from you?
- What do you do for them that others can't?
- Are their needs and motivations changing?
- Are you still addressing what they want as well as ever?

Every business has its risks – even water companies with no visible competition to worry about have to ensure they keep their promises to watchdogs and don't fall foul of public opinion. Most businesses, however, have much more than that to think about, operating as they do in open marketplaces with competition on all sides. And there are many examples out there of successful companies that have lost their way simply because they didn't keep up with their markets and with the changing needs of their customers.

Who are we thinking of? From recent history, the record label and record shop business HMV is a good example – it failed to adapt quickly enough to the demands of the digital age and paid the price, while online rivals like iTunes mopped up.

Or there's the equally telling example of Kodak. In 2012, the 124-year-old manufacturer of film and cameras filed for bankruptcy protection in the USA, following many years of negative financial returns. Just five years earlier, in 2007, its stock price was $90 per share. In January of 2012 that had sunk to 76 cents. What happened? What hadn't happened, more like. As customers began to enjoy digital images and digital cameras in numbers, Kodak's management stayed the course with the company's traditional film and camera lines. They believed Kodak's customer base would never desert the company. Say no more.

Before we move on, here's another example to ponder from further back: the railways in the USA made their owners rich and powerful in the decades at the end of the nineteenth and the beginning of the twentieth century – but in just a few short years spanning the 1950s and 1960s the industry was all but wiped out by roads and by lorries. Why didn't those business-owners understand what was happening and do something about it? Partly because they could not see that their business was transportation rather than railways. By not seeing roads and trucks as a threat they missed the big picture – and their businesses were turned upside-down in quick time.

Forget loyalty

Half a century on from that particular business apocalypse, some will still tell you that customer loyalty counts today and is worth cherishing. As you might have guessed by now, we don't agree: loyalty is an illusion – a false interpretation that some will project on a customer that's still buying. (Just ask Kodak's former board members what they think about loyalty now!)

If you really believe that customers will stay loyal to your brand simply out of habit or comfort or personal loyalties, it's time to think again. Brand loyalty has never been more than weak in most contexts – and even that is disappearing fast in today's transforming world. There are more ways of finding and buying products or services than ever before, and it has changed the competitive landscape for good.

What are you selling?

Harley-Davidson is not selling a vehicle for transportation but something much less tangible – it's selling the promise of freedom out on the open road.

Revlon might make lipstick in its factories, but its boss once said that in the shops what the company sells is hope.

Apply that same sort of thinking to what your company sells: get beyond the functional purpose and ask yourself what satisfaction you deliver for your customers, because that's the true value proposition of your business.

Working this out matters not just to the extent that it enables you to target your customers better – that's a part of it, of course, but only a part. It affects everything, and especially the price that customers are prepared to pay.

The consumer market is, as ever, good for examples that illustrate the point. No one ever bought a Rolls-Royce for its functional ability to transport people from A to B. No one ever ate in a top-end restaurant in order to consume enough calories to stay alive. The satisfactions of luxury cars and fancy restaurants – and the value that people see in these propositions – have everything to do with intangibles like the sense of exclusivity and specialness that is wrapped up in the experience.

Many of the businesses we help at Business Doctors sell to businesses rather than consumers, and often have several different types of customer to please. But the same principles apply as for the big consumer brands that put so much time, energy and resource into getting the proposition and 'brand' right – understand what you are selling, and to whom, make sure you reach them in the best and most cost-effective ways, and make sure you deliver every time.

Before we look more closely at how to get this challenge right, let's turn it around. How do companies get it wrong?

The mistakes people make:
MISUNDERSTANDING WHAT YOU SELL

We'll begin with an example from the legal sector. One common mistake we see here is firms trying to sell the legal transaction rather than the satisfaction a successful transaction will provide. Many legal jobs – think probate or property conveyancing – are necessities that most people want to see sorted out painlessly and efficiently so they can enjoy the sensation of a problem or obligation solved.

What the law firms should be selling therefore – and many still don't – is the satisfaction you can get from engaging a personable legal expert who is on your side and getting things done. People want to know there is someone in their corner 'protecting their interests' as the formula has it. It may cost money, but the idea is that it's worth it because having the lawyer on your side holds the promise of avoiding eye-watering costs and risks down the line – and of arguments being resolved before they even begin. Similarly with a project like creating a will, which is an uncomfortable thing for anyone to have to sort out, what surely needs to be sold is the fuzzy feeling that a person will get from protecting their family and loved ones from all eventualities.

Before we move on, here's another classic mistake from the world of law (and all these issues have the same root, remember, of failing to recognize what the customer is really buying). We've seen plenty of lawyers down the years with customer literature that confidently reassures the would-be client that they will be seeing a 'fee-earner' from the get-go. A fee-earner is of course an internal label in professional firms for the experts that provide value by delivering the service to 'earn the fee', so you can see how the mistake gets made. But plenty of would-be customers who are already jittery about engaging expensive lawyers might run a mile at mention of a 'fee-earner' being wheeled out from the very first meeting. It makes the whole process sound scarily expensive!

The mistakes people make: CHARGING THAT IGNORES CUSTOMER VALUE

In some sectors the challenge lies in how to charge the customer for a service, because the results run the risk of not bearing much relation to the fee that's due. If that sounds counterintuitive, consider the world of public relations, where sometimes a single phone call to the right journalist at the right time with the right proposition will yield more value than several weeks of effort elsewhere. How do you charge your client in such a context? Well, plenty in the PR world have ignored the outputs side of that equation and focused squarely on the hours worked. While that might make sense from the point of view of the agency's profit-and-loss account, it's hardly customer-focused! Nowadays more and more PR firms are acknowledging this, offering payment-by-results where they feel that they can, although the hours-worked model is still used by most.

The mistakes people make: YOUR OWN AGENDA, NOT YOUR CUSTOMER'S

Have you ever set foot in a restaurant only to be met by a waiter who wants to know the purpose of your visit?

'Are you here for breakfast or lunch, sir?'

Is there a right or wrong answer here? There shouldn't be – and it's a terrible place to start up any relationship with a new customer.

Why? Because people go to restaurants to enjoy themselves and have some fun – not to be made to feel like a problem in the making. Sure, some restaurants might run separate morning and lunchtime menus, but for someone waiting to be seated that really shouldn't be a concern. It's up to the restaurant to accommodate the customer and make them feel comfortable – not the other way around.

Here's another example we heard about from the restaurant trade, along similar lines.

Some customers were talking across two tables in a restaurant and asked the server if they could pull the two tables together. In a few minutes, the manager came by and said it wasn't possible: the tables were arranged so that each one would be lit in a certain way, and so they never move the tables. 'We don't really care about the lighting,' was the response, but the restaurant manager wouldn't budge, and no alternative was explored. Instead all the customers got was: 'No. We don't want to do that, because it's not what we want to do.'

In effect, the restaurant manager was saying: our lighting scheme is more important to us than our customers' happiness.

Who would return to such a restaurant?

Who is the customer again?

Every corner of business has its particular nuances in terms of the customer. And many companies that sell to other businesses rather than consumers have several customer types to worry about.

If you are a manufacturer making tools for home hobbyists, the business will mostly sell through distributors – who are your direct customers – but the ultimate users of your products are those individual consumers. So you've two kinds of relationship to think about: one direct and one indirect (with perhaps some direct selling through your website in the mix too).

Or consider the commercial radio station – or indeed many print and online publishers. There are two customer types here as well: the listener (or magazine reader or site visitor) and the advertiser. The challenge is that having more than one type of customer to deliver for can lead to tensions or do damage to a business when one type is prioritized over another without good reason.

Recruitment consultants are yet another example in this space. Their proposition needs to appeal to would-be job candidates and to the companies that are recruiting.

We are sure you get the picture! The point we are making is that business is often complex, and it's all too easy for companies to fail to grasp their core purpose – and therefore to fail to understand their core customers.

Think through the opportunity

Any attempt to understand the customer can usefully start with a brain-storming session among the company leadership, perhaps facilitated by someone who sits outside of the business.

It makes sense to start by looking at the market and at the wider opportunities for growth. Which opportunities are relevant – and why? Which really aren't? (And again – why not?)

And what do we mean by the 'wider market'?

It's simple. If you are an estate agent, you aren't just in property sales but in the market for services around property. If you run a hair-dressing salon then you are in the beauty and feel-good business: you could equally have a nail bar or offer Botox alongside the hairstyling if that's the right way to take things.

Clarity is what you are after here. Describe what the customer is buying from you in as much useful detail as possible. Why do they buy it? What needs are you satisfying? What really matters in terms of their decision-making? In short, you need to **THINK LIKE THE CUSTOMER** and stop thinking about yourself and your business.

Once you embark on this approach you should soon start to see some of the things you have been missing. And very quickly it might well change how you sell and position and communicate about your product or service.

Events can bring you closer to customers. Events are one way to bring you face-to-face with your customers – which is where you need to be to understand their true desires, fears and challenges. (In other words, their real needs.)

Events help you sell to customers. If you want to sell to your customers or prospective customers, try events. At events, rapport is developed almost immediately. And, when there are a lot of attendees, you gain social proof and popularity. And at most events the energy level is high. Attendees are excited to get away from the day-to-day and are more eager to sign up for the new programme, product or service you offer.

Events give you testimonials. Because the energy level is so high and positive at most events, you can get great written, audio and/or video testimonials from attendees. Post these on your website or put them in your other marketing materials and they will help you secure additional customers.

Events invigorate your staff. Events also get your staff out of their daily element. Staff members get to interact with customers and see that the work they do on a daily basis is positively impacting others.

Stop selling

It's time to be really explicit. One thing that everyone in your company who is charged with business development or sales should do right away, if they haven't already, is to **STOP SELLING!** The days of the hard sell are over. People don't want to be sold to. They want to be consulted with by experts who want to hear about their needs in as much detail as they can provide. If a customer or would-be customer feels you are there to satisfy them, it will make them confident that whatever you do end up suggesting is based on what they want and need. They truly will trust you to deliver.

Building up trust is a core principle that runs through the whole book. And at Business Doctors we apply that same thinking to how we operate. When we work with any client, we are there to listen and to help the business leader formulate their own story – and that should be your approach to your customers too. When a meeting reaches its natural conclusion, your customer should want you to help and support them – that's the quality of trust you should be aspiring towards.

Real world example: The cabling company

We worked with director of a cabling company who undertook a root-and-branch overhaul of the business.

One part of the journey he went on was to understand the customer and what they were buying from him.

He originally thought his customers were buying his company's technical expertise and its particular product sets. But our work with him soon found that primarily what they were buying was the confidence that their businesses wouldn't be disrupted.

The company had built up a customer base in a niche that saw it mainly working with law firms. What these firms were doing when they engaged his business was setting up new offices and moving existing ones. Above all else they wanted to feel confident that these plans would not affect the day-to-day running of their firm – and so that's what the company needed to start selling. It needed to tell its would-be customers that the move they were considering would be safe and seamless, with limited downtime, if they chose them.

Get ready to feel transformed

So what will happen to the business if you work hard at understanding your customers and approach every customer meeting this way? A transformation, that's what.

Our experience is that many smaller businesses are not good at focusing on customer need and at engaging customers in the right way. Once they start to do so, opportunities will often open up for them.

One reason for this is that the process helps many small-business owners to understand for the first time, and with real clarity, their point of differentiation in the marketplace – really enabling them to start to compete!

Very few small businesses are competing on price, after all. It's bigger companies that have the scale that enables them to drive down costs and keep margins tight. But luckily enough it doesn't matter! What's great about being small in business is that 99% of buying decisions are not price-sensitive in any case. Price comes up a lot in conversations and is used as an excuse by sales people who aren't closing deals, but most of the time the issue will actually lie elsewhere (normally in not talking to the customer in the right way!).

The customer conversation

One thing you'll be excited to discover is that customers are only too happy to talk not just about their needs but also to cast a useful critical eye on your business proposition and how it delivers (or comes up short) for them.

Believe us, it's true! And so it makes sense to start asking! In these conversations the customers are still obliquely talking about themselves, remember, so you aren't breaking any 'rules' here. Just get asking:

- Why do you buy from us?
- What do you like or dislike about what we do?
- What do you really value?
- What other products or services might you like to buy from us if you could?

Is this market research you are conducting? Yes and no. It's more useful in some respects, giving you real insights you can act on, but it won't necessarily answer some questions that would require a more analytical approach. It's qualitative research rather than quantitative, if you like.

What's certain is that it will take you on a journey that's worth travelling. It will help you clarify what business you are in – and help you to sell. It will enable you to forge stronger relationships with your customers. It will help you articulate your core purpose in a few words, to be the benefit of your staff and your suppliers and your customers.

And it will start you on a journey that will give you a vision for the future. But more of that in the next chapter.

Know your customer, serve your customer

1. **Customers value 'good' service over fast service.** 15 minutes in paradise is better than 5 minutes in hell, every time.

2. **Customer like to feel special.** One study in the restaurant industry found that waiters received tips nearly a quarter higher on average if they delivered a second set of mints to customers after presenting the bill. It's that easy to make people feel special.

3. **Customers can help you innovate.** A recent study of nearly 1,200 successful innovations across nine industries showed that 60% originated from customers and customer feedback.

4. **Tell a good story.** Time and again research shows that a well-told story is one of the most persuasive forms of writing – or speaking – there is. Stories

transport the listener to another place, enabling companies to deliver a powerful message that sticks.

5. **Surprise them!** One of the most lasting and talked about customer experiences is a pleasant surprise. Do something nice for your customers that they really don't expect and good things will surely come of it.

Chapter 5

Are you ready to break big?

Does a business need a vision? Isn't it a bit pie-in-the-sky to start talking about what a company will look like in five or ten years' time, especially given the economic uncertainties in the air these days? And with day-to-day issues to handle, it's surely extremely hard to come up with anything truly visionary that will stand the test of time . . .

This isn't what we think, don't worry. Not for a minute. But it's what plenty of people think and say – and they couldn't be more wrong.

This is what we think.

We think every business needs its leaders to set some visionary goals to aspire to and live by – and that's what this chapter is all about. It doesn't matter if forecasting or modelling for the business can only be done with confidence or accuracy over shorter time frames – 6 or 12 or 18 months, say. The need for a real long-term vision is still crucial. And here's something that might surprise you: it's immediately relevant too, since putting in place a vision will affect certain decisions and choices from day one onwards.

But why do we say you need a vision? Partly it's because a leader setting a challenging goal is the best way to get a business moving in the right direction, whatever the pessimism or lack of ambition that others may express. No one, for example, could ever accuse Facebook's Mark Zuckerberg of lacking a vision and some cast-iron self-belief, and it has got Facebook a long way in a short time.

Our point is that the perceived wisdom about what's possible and what's not is mostly defined by what has gone before – and that's no indicator of what's achievable and what isn't. Whatever else you do, therefore, you should try to aim high and keep dreaming. If you do, every company really does have the potential to be transformed – and to break big!

Avoiding invisible limits

When it comes to human habits, it's a sad fact that most people behave like fleas in jar.

If you put some fleas in a jar, they jump up and down and quickly learn how high they should jump to avoid bumping against the lid of the jar. If you later remove that lid, the fleas don't jump any higher. They've conditioned themselves only to jump a certain height, lid or no lid. They've set a limit on themselves, and unconsciously decided what's possible.

Establishing a vision is one way of breaking free of that sort of limited mindset.

What should this vision look like then? A visionary goal should potentially be achievable further down the line but not be something that's possible in the short term. It should strive for something more than the current reality and not be limiting at all.

So what is a visionary goal not? It's certainly not a version of a business plan or a strategy document. It's not rooted in forecasts or incremental year-on-year gains. It's a big idea that sets the bar high.

Thinking big – Amazon

Talking of big ideas, here's a perfect example to get you thinking big.

In 1994 Jeff Bezos was already extremely successful. Only just 30, he was the youngest-ever senior vice president at a Wall Street investment bank, with a big salary and great career prospects. But Jeff had a vision for the then-fledgling internet – online retailing – and quit his comfortable, high-achieving job.

Bezos first got the idea to start what became Amazon when he came across a statistic in the early 1990s that said internet usage was growing by 2,300% a month.

He could see which way the wind was blowing and the potential for selling online, so he drew up a list of 20 potential products he thought might sell well via the internet, including software, CDs and books. After further analysis, he saw that books were the obvious place to start because of the number of titles in existence. Bezos realized that while even the largest superstores could stock only a few hundred thousand books, an online bookstore could offer millions of titles.

Armed with this idea, he raised the first $1 m of investment in what became Amazon from family and friends and went from there, working out of the garage of a rented a house in Seattle.

It took a year for Bezos and a crew of five employees to get somewhere meaningful, learning between them how to source books and establishing an online platform that would make Amazon.com easy to navigate. And built into the vision from the off was the need for a user-friendly interface that would streamline the often random process of bookstore shopping by providing a 'virtual community' for visitors, enabling visitor-generated book reviews and more.

By July 1995 Amazon was launched. It was even able at launch to style itself 'Earth's biggest book store' and was immediately successful, fuelled by its enormous selection of books, superior customer service and that user-friendly site design.

By September 1996 Amazon had already grown into a company of 100 employees and racked up more than $15.7m in sales. In a further three years those figures had rocketed to more than 3,000 employees, including some in the UK and Germany, and more than $610m in sales.

The rest, as they say, is history: Amazon has been innovating ever since and is still headed by the restless Bezos, whose obsession with delivering for the customer and whose analytics-driven vision has helped to make the company a world leader.

Vision, of course, lies at the heart of what Bezos has created with Amazon. He was thinking big from the beginning, looking to create a business of huge potential and scale, even if he knew it couldn't happen overnight. But it was that vision that the original employees were buying into when they started working for the pre-commercial Amazon – and it must have been an exciting place to work even then, when the business proper was still just an idea.

The leader's vision

We hope you can see from this example how a business vision and the need for strong business leadership are two sides of the same coin. Many successful businesses are driven by visionaries who can see through the limitations of negativity and don't allow anything to upset their own self-belief and belief in the organization they are creating. Often it is their passion, as expressed in a vision, that will glue everyone together to work towards a shared goal.

For some, of course, this is instinctive stuff: it's part of their DNA as leaders – and the organization benefits as it is carried along with them.

For others, providing this kind of inspired leadership isn't so instinctive, but no matter: it can be worked on and developed as a shared goal to inspire the leader and everyone else to strive.

The good news, too, is that the benefits of embracing and developing a vision are even more likely to be felt in smaller businesses than in big corporates. Why? Simply because so many small businesses only account for a tiny fraction of market share, which means that whatever is going on in the market or the wider economy shouldn't really affect the company vision and whether it's achievable. If you are a £2m turnover business gunning for £20m in a UK market worth £1bn, say, whether the market is growing or shrinking marginally is not really a constraining factor when it comes to that big goal.

The believer and the non-believer

Let's stop briefly here and share an example that illustrates something more about business vision and what it should look like.

We were called in to work with a public relations business run by two equal shareholders. One was a larger-than-life character who always talked in grand terms when we spoke about the business – about million-pound deals and huge opportunities that were poised to come off. The other director, somewhat unusually given her business partner, was financially savvy and ultra-cautious about prospects. As personalities they really were chalk and cheese.

The company was relatively small, turning over about £300,000 a year, but operating in a PR niche that was growing rapidly in the UK. It led the ultra-positive partner to talk about growing the business to £10m quite quickly. The trouble was, no one else in the company – and particularly not his fellow shareholder – believed him or bought the vision. It seemed too unattainable and rooted in his boasting and bullishness.

It was our job to find a middle ground that satisfied these two very different characters: a vision that they could both buy into that fed the dreams of the dreamer while satisfying the cautious partner about the essential truth of the goal being set.

It was challenging, as you can imagine, but we found relatively quickly that there was a vision to be drawn out that both business partners found they could draw on. More than that, it was ambitious, too! It targeted £15m of turnover on the basis of the myriad opportunities we could all agree on once we worked things through.

Armed with this new goal, the company never quite got to £15m, but it did reach £5.7m turnover before the two founders went their separate ways – and that wasn't a failure, by any means. Growing from £300k turnover to £5.7m is something to be proud of, for sure. And it was made possible by harnessing the creativity and optimism of the one partner and lifting the lid on the jar that was holding back the other.

What should be drawn from the story? First, that visions need to be believable – and then believed! – if they are to motivate and inspire. Second, that once you start planning around being a bigger business, great things will often flow from that – and quickly. Just because the big-vision partner was sometimes unrealistic about prospects, it didn't mean he was far off target. Some of the deals he kept talking about when we first showed up really did come off – maybe not quite as described, but convincingly enough to take the business from a minnow to a decent-sized player in this particular marketplace in just a couple of years.

Why you must live the vision

A vision that your company starts to live by will carry it a long way.

If you plan for your business to be small, it will be. If you plan for your business to be big, it doesn't follow that you will reach your goal – but it does mean you'll apply the logic of that goal in all your decisions. That will create the best chance for your company to deliver on its potential in the marketplace.

This is because a true vision isn't just something you talk about but something you live by every day. And it's an important point, so we'll take our time here.

Imagine your vision is to grow the company from £1m to £7m turnover within five years. Before you even get started on that journey, the next step is to imagine what a £7m-turnover version of the company will look like. How many staff will it have, and with what skills? How much space will it need? Where might it need offices? What technologies will it be using? What partners will it have? What leadership team will it need in place to run effectively?

You need to think about this **NOW**, not just as a flight of fancy but because a business that's turning over seven times more will look different to today's company, and getting there will be a journey. It's a journey that needs to start at once.

Just stop to think. As companies grow they need more structures in place if they are to work well. They need a management team with complementary skills, for starters. Someone to run the finances, someone to look after HR issues, someone to drive operational matters, someone to develop new business, perhaps someone to oversee IT needs. These are requirements that can't be fulfilled overnight but need to be worked towards – usually over several years.

Having a vision, in other words, gives you a framework for how the business will run from here. It should inform what happens each and every day, because no one creates a big, successful business by accident. You need the intent and a structured plan too.

Some business leaders, and particularly serial entrepreneurs who have been there and done it, know this and apply the logic from the moment they start a business. Some even have an exit strategy in mind, and how to get from here to there.

Most don't, however. As we've touched on elsewhere, entrepreneurs and business leaders come in all shapes and sizes, and a good proportion don't think that way at all. Some are excited by the process of creating something from nothing and tend to fall down on some of the detail and attention to needed for sustainable growth. Others start a business because they can see the market opportunity, but then get bogged down in the day-to-day. There are many variations on the theme, of course, but it seems safe to say that, among the millions of small businesses here in the UK, only a minority – and a small one at that – are run by leaders who have got all the bases covered from start to finish.

Time to get started

At first it can be shocking when you begin to think about the current business structure and compare it with the kind of structure that will be needed to sustain a bigger company. All of those new systems and processes and locations and people to support can look overwhelming.

But once you start to break things down everything will soon look quite different. After all, getting a company from £1m to £7m turnover, as in our example, won't need seven times more staff or seven times more suppliers or seven times more space – or seven times more anything, in all likelihood.

That's one of the beauties of business – economies of scale mean you will be more efficient as you start to grow (and particularly if you are already established and aren't trying to get from three to ten staff, where profitability doesn't always improve smoothly with staffing and investment). A £1.2m turnover business might employ 15 staff, but to get to £6m might only take 30 staff. It's not an easy evolution, and will take time, but the effort really is repaid in most cases.

And, of course, it's the vision that gets everything moving. Put simply, being on a road somewhere requires a destination: planned evolution is the aim rather than stumbling forwards in search of 'organic' growth.

Taking those first steps

Once you've started on this journey there should be no reason to turn back. Suddenly feel like you need a sales director, having never had one? Of course you do! But one step at a time.

Working with your vision in mind at all times should make you purposeful on all fronts, because it will affect everything. For starters, it will affect your relationships with customers and suppliers and with staff – and mostly for the better. But everything new has its challenges, too. This is a change that will affect how you think about all your relationships and probably what many of them think about you.

Making a splash

My first ever business investment was in a radio station. One of the co-investors was Tom Bloxham, the co-founder and chairman of the development company Urban Splash – and someone who has always embraced thinking big. He brought me in as MD but on one non-negotiable basis – I had to make a significant financial commitment to the business. (In fact, that's something I now recommend to any business founders bringing in an MD.)

It felt like a big risk at the time, but Tom in particular encouraged me to see the opportunity rather than the potential downsides. It was a powerful part of the company culture and made it all the easier to commit to the business 100%. The vision all along was clear: we can make this happen, the company will strive for excellence and have a high-achieving culture, and it will be financially rewarding.

The project proved to be challenging and rewarding, and we eventually sold out to a much bigger radio group. The lessons I learnt about commitment and having a big vision were crucial and have stayed with me ever since.

Matt

Consider when you are recruiting staff, even at a relatively junior level. All of sudden you've got this story to tell about where the company is headed and how you plan to get there. That's just the kind of idea likely to get would-be employees excited, isn't it? It probably also helps you stand out from the competition that your would-be staffer may also be talking to. And the real beauty of it, assuming you've fully committed, is that it's absolutely true! You **ARE** on this journey with this particular, ambitious goal in mind – and anyone that joins should want to buy into that.

Suppliers will notice as well. Some business-to-business supplier relationships are arm's length and transactional, but here's a chance to refresh things and put them on a different footing. From the supplier company's perspective, being a small supplier to a £1m turnover company that's treading water is one sort of relationship. Being a supplier to an ambitious company that's planning shortly to extend itself into new markets with new products and services, and to be at £5m or £10m turnover within a few years, is a different sort of profile. It's one that may be worth fully engaging with and supporting in new ways. Equally, with the shoe on the other foot, you may come to realize that some existing suppliers might not be right for your business as it grows and new relationships may need to be established.

Partner companies are also likely to get excited over where the company is headed and what it might mean by extension for their business. They might commit to some new projects, and deepen the relationship all round for both sides' mutual benefit.

And then there are the customers. If it's a B2B business, some of these might now be inclined to view the business more like a potential partner – or just to do more business all around. If the customer or potential customer is in the public sector then it might be the difference between being able to bid for some work or not. For example, if in a tender bid you are able to describe how your company will look if you win the work rather than how it looks now, it could put you on a different footing entirely.

Moving on up

Clearly there are risks that will be taken on this growth journey: in the case of public tenders, you don't want to over-promise or over-extend yourself in a way that some would view as fraudulent. But equally there are great opportunities as you start to grow. In some ways the world of business gets easier as you move up a level or two. Some of the competition actually thins out as you grow. There are often better, longer contracts up for grabs, with better pricing relative to your own costs, and work that lets you plan ahead and invest with more confidence than ever. And there are new customers that you can go after that were previously out of reach because you didn't fit their supplier profile.

In short, things can start happening quickly. It's that much easier to raise finance, for one thing – a huge sticking point for many smaller companies, we hardly need to tell you.

If those are some of the external dynamics that are changing as the company grows, what about how things will change within the business?

One crucial area, connected with external recruitment of course, lies in staff development. One of the most immediate impacts of living your business vision will be on the people in the business, on the approach to finding new hires and on the thorny issue of succession planning.

Having a vision to live by should be great for staff motivation, but it will also require you to make bigger calls when it comes to staffing. Who should you try to develop to step up into more senior roles – even boardroom roles? How can you hold onto the best people for longer, since losing them could damage the business? Should you create another tier of well-paid senior management to ensure all the growth you are seeing and targeting can be serviced? Can you keep the same culture and positivity in the business if it is growing rapidly?

Tweaking the vision

These and other important questions will need to be addressed with confidence if you are to make the most of all the positivity being created by your vision. One of the challenges created by establishing a vision, in fact, is finding the means by which you can work back from the vision and apply it to some of the detail of the business from day to day and week to week.

Once you start to implement change, working on today, tomorrow and next week from within the business, the challenge becomes how you ensure that all the steps you are taking are in keeping with the business vision – and even whether it needs a rewrite as the business takes shape.

One way to embrace these changes is to track quite systematically which choices you are taking that are informed by the vision, so that the sense of purpose and progress is made even more real. You can also review the vision as part of this process, revising targets upwards where you feel confident enough to do so.

Ignore the knock-backs

For some who embark on the journey we've begun to describe, their confidence is unshakeable. There's a particular type of serial entrepreneur who has been there and done it all before and doesn't let anything dent self-belief.

For the rest of us, it's natural to doubt yourself to some extent when something doesn't go to plan. Equally it's important to keep to the long-term plan and to understand that losing the occasional battle doesn't mean you won't win through in the end.

When something doesn't work out, our advice is to try hard to keep your eyes on the destination and not to sweat the small stuff. On occasion, it's true that the 'small stuff' won't be all that small – something might be going properly awry. But if so you should still try hard to learn the lesson and regroup. You should also try to ensure there is enough fat in the business to cushion it from any lasting issues – and that all the risks you are taking are in some way reversible.

What do we mean by that last point? Well, here's a simple example. One drinks business client we have been working with is poised to take on someone in a senior branding role to help develop the business. At the time of writing we cannot say with absolute confidence that the appointment will work out for this client and pay its way, even if there are good grounds for optimism. One contingency that the company has needed to cover, therefore, is the chance that it doesn't quite work out – so we've convinced the client to put a layoff clause in the initial employment contract as a just-in-case move. We don't believe the company will need it, but it's there all the same. It's one less thing for the company's owners to think about.

Seven steps towards your company vision

1. **Define your vision.** A vision can be used for every aspect of a business, so start by being clear about what you're working on. You'll want a vision for the organization overall but also very likely for particular pieces. Do you want a vision for the medium term and the long term too? They might be a bit different. You can and should have lots of visions – wherever you need them to focus on what matters.

2. **Pick a timeframe.** How far out should you look? There's no right answer, but as a general principle, visioning works best if you go far out enough to get beyond present-day problems but not so far out that you have no sense at all of actually getting there. Most organizational visions will probably be set somewhere from two to ten years out—but five is a typical place to start.

3. **Put together a list of 'prouds'.** Get down a list of past achievements. You might include specific contributions that you or your colleagues have made to past successes, or skills, techniques and resources that could be assets in achieving your vision. Anything good that comes to mind is fine. It shouldn't take more than ten minutes. The idea is just to create a base of positive energy and high-quality experiences on which you can build future success. The more people focus on the positives, the more likely you are to attain the greatness you envision.

4. **Write that draft.** Writing a vision is hugely important. Before you start writing, here are a few tips:

- Put something wild out there. Get past the 59 reasons why it won't work.

- Put down what pours out, not what other people want to see.

- Write as if your vision has already happened.

- Keep writing for 15 to 30 minutes, regardless of how silly you sound.

- Build your passions into what you write. Don't write a vision that you aren't a part of.

5. **Do some more redrafts.** When you're ready to revise, read your draft through from start to finish. Don't get rid of anything. You'll have plenty of opportunity to edit the content and the language. As you read through, keep in the back of your mind: Does this sound inspiring? Do I get excited when I'm reading it? Stay away from vague statements like 'We're busier than ever'; instead, use real sales numbers that mean something. What are the key financial numbers that define success for you? Use those.

6. **Get some input.** This is where you let the cat out of the bag and get input from people you trust and respect. Whom should you show it to? Folks who have experience, insight and expertise relevant to your vision. Inevitably, some of these advisors will shift away from talking about the vision into a discussion of the action steps that will have to be in a strategic plan. Just listen carefully, and take notes – some of those ideas might come in handy later.

7. **Share the vision.** Eventually you'll be ready to share the vision with everyone who will be involved in

implementing it. When you roll out your vision to the bigger group, people will ask questions about how you intend to achieve the vision. They're asking you about the how. The vision, however, is the what. It's totally fine if you don't know how you're going to get there. Later on you can figure out the how.

Part Two

KNOW YOUR OPPORTUNITIES

For anyone in business, a little knowledge is a dangerous thing. To thrive, what businesses need is A LOT of knowledge. That way everyone understands just which opportunities to go after (and why) and which to ignore. Knowledge takes many forms, of course. There are the external realities to grasp, as we do in Chapter 6, but also work that needs to go into understanding the business better to ensure it's delivering just what customers need (and preferably that the competitors don't).

Chapter 6

What's the big picture?

Doing some hard thinking about the context that your business inhabits, in order to protect it against what's around the corner, shouldn't feel overwhelming. Really.

Why do we begin things by saying that? Because we know from first-hand experience with business leaders that this kind of boardroom session – looking at the big picture in economic and social and political and technological terms – is sometimes greeted by groans and head-scratching from those around the table.

It's the idea of piling into loads of theory that ruffles people's feathers. Those who create and run businesses are often pragmatic and hands-on types who shy away from anything too cerebral or academic.

The good news, however, is that any instinct entrepreneurs might have to avoid getting analytical about the wider context their business inhabits is well wide of mark. Once you start to dig a little, and explore all the external factors that are out there, there is invariably a huge amount to think about and to talk through. It's usually interesting, stimulating and exciting!

Snakes and ladders

If the early chapters of the book were all about trying to develop the best understanding of the **DESTINATION** for your business, the next few are more granular, exploring on-the-ground issues and external factors. And this chapter has one simple focus: it explores how you unpick and analyze the **EXTERNAL OPPORTUNITIES AND RISKS** that the business might face along the way. When we tackle it with business leaders we sometimes start by talking about the 'snakes and ladders' that are out there to get across something of what's involved.

What the chapter is **NOT** is an analysis of the internal resource that's in the business that you could tap to do things better. That's something that's coming in Chapter 7. Instead, this is self-consciously a chance to look at what is happening in the wider world, **OUTSIDE** of the business, that could impact upon it.

Just like in the children's board game, ladders refer to any opportunities that could help to jump-start the business by opening up new areas for sales or helping to improve profit margins. Snakes, meanwhile, are those changes in the social, political, economic and technological space that might restrict the business in some way, perhaps by taking away a problem that the business was solving or by introducing competition that radically cuts or even removes margins. In the most extreme cases, you might end up analyzing a threat with the potential to wipe out the business in its current form. It can – and does – happen.

One further thing to say here is that the starting point for this chapter presupposes that enough work in grounding the business has been done. All of the **DESTINATION** work we covered in various ways in Chapters 1 to 5: the need for inspiration and self-analysis by those in the boardroom, and the development of the values and vision for the business, as well as the need to understand just what the business is about and how it needs to be structured to succeed. It's once you feel that this is taken care of that you can really start to consider the boosters and pitfalls that might be waiting for your business over the next horizon.

Setting things up

These **EXPLORATION** chapters of the book are also a chance to sanity-check how feasible some of your thinking about the business and its ultimate destination really is. Is the bar being set too low or too high? Is there rapid growth potential for the business that you haven't factored in or properly understood? Or could the whole thing be undermined by something so far unforeseen?

When working with clients, we often call this an exercise in **FUTURE-PROOFING**, and those four headline factors we tend to work with – social, economic, technological and political – are well-used when looking at the external (or macro-environmental) realities, though there are plenty of variations out there too.

Some approaches collect up the headlines and call this a PEST analysis (political, economic, social and technological analysis), while others add legal to the mix and rearrange the mnemonic to SLEPT. Other still insert environmental factors into the list as its own heading, giving them PESTEL or PESTLE to work with – or even STEEPLE and STEEPLED once ethics and demographic factors are included. Or STEER is another take on the same, using socio-cultural, technological, economic, ecological, and regulatory factors as the headings.

Don't worry, it doesn't matter too much which of these you use, but some context is useful to have. We happen to think four headings is just fine, as the headlines are broad enough not to miss anything out and will help to give you a focus and a strategic tool for understanding your business position, its potential and the best likely direction for operations.

Putting the theory into practice

Once you start to apply this analysis to any business, it will soon get you thinking.

Let's start quite simply, with one client we had that was active in the renewable energy sector, installing and maintaining solar panels and offering consultancy services too.

It's a nice example because there are so many external factors for a business like this to weigh:

- **SOCIAL:** In social terms, solar energy has cachet since it is a renewable energy that can help reduce the UK's dependency on fossil fuels, the use of which contributes to global warming. As an industry, it's extremely socially acceptable and investible because of its environmental credentials – and it's reasonable to expect renewables to continue to be seen as socially responsible, even if the technologies keep evolving and changing. In the UK, there is widespread acceptance of the social need to adopt renewable energy as a response to the dangers of global warming, with dissenting voices only at the margins.

- **TECHNOLOGICAL:** Improvements in the efficiency of solar panels are making the industry more attractive all the time, as the viability of solar as a reliable means of energy production and hence as an investment is stacking up better and better. Also improvements in metering technologies mean that metering of electricity usage and of input into the UK's national electricity grid is improving all the time, transforming the landscape for electricity micro-generation.

- **ECONOMIC:** The economic case for renewables has been on the up for many years, as the price of non-renewable fuel is volatile and as a general trend keeps on increasing relative to income, while the cost of renewable micro-generation continues to improve relative to upfront costs. These days it's still the case that most UK electricity is produced by burning oil, natural gas or coal. These are risky, bumpy markets in some respects and cutting exposure to them is seen as a good means of reducing economic risks.

- **POLITICAL:** The UK government has supported renewable energy with various financial incentives for a few years now. The government will continue to support the industry, it seems reasonable to assume, given its commitment to reducing the UK's carbon dioxide emissions. By 2020 the aim is to generate 20% of all UK electric supply via renewal sources of energy and by 2050 to have cut carbon dioxide emissions by 80% for the UK compared with 1990 levels.

Any analysis like this could be a lot more detailed – and focused more precisely on the nuances of the individual business – but we are sure you get the idea.

We've also left out one crucial nugget, which is that, although most of the external factors related to solar energy have made it look an attractive area for businesses, it is also a sector that has seen dramatic changes in government support and state subsidies. The main mechanism for UK subsidy around small-scale electricity generation has been the Feed-In Tariff, but the qualification criteria for the subsidies has changed more than once since FIT launched, and the subsidy levels themselves have also changed. Each such change has altered the landscape for the industry by changing the market dynamics overnight – not an easy thing for a company to plan for, but something that every business in the sector has needed to grasp.

Old industry, new look

If solar energy production is a relatively young mass industry, and hence might be expected to see dramatic changes in the external factors that affect it, no industry or business is immune from change in the wider world.

Consider the legal sector – a bastion of old-schoolism and frankly uncompetitive working practices until recently, but not for much longer. A few years ago, any law firm with a bit of ambition that was looking at the external opportunities and threats coming its way will have tried to understand what changes the UK's Legal Services Act would usher in with its opening up of law firm ownership to non-lawyers and general liberalizing of a previously closed and staid market.

The changes, which came into force on October 2011, were radical enough in themselves, allowing the likes of Co-op Group to move into legal services provision. And when combined with the rapid technological and social developments being enabled by the internet and by changes in mobile technology, the overall change to the sector has been profound and disruptive. In a 2013 report, 18 months on from the Legal Services Act becoming law, a quarter of law firms said they expected to change their business strategy because of the act – up from 9% in 2010 – and the sector has seen plenty of consolidation as many less dynamic firms have been acquired.

The retail revolution

If law is a sector that has been hit by a storm of change in a relatively short period in the UK, then in retailing across the world there has been nothing short of a hurricane.

It's not legislative change that has transformed this broad-based sector but technological change ushering in social change on a grand scale.

Amazon has been one high-profile winner in this space, but there are winners and losers every day and week and month in every corner of retailing around the world.

What's changed in retail? Nearly everything. These days, retail doesn't just mean shops on the high street plus a bit of catalogue shopping. It is now conducted through multiple channels, including traditional retail stores, online stores, mobile stores, mobile app stores, interactive television, telephone hotlines and plenty of other weird and sometimes wonderful ways of transacting with a customer. Amazon and eBay have become the world's virtual shop fronts in their own right, and in 2013 more and more of this business is beginning to take place through mobile devices like smartphones and tablets.

Who saw it all coming? Well, no one could have predicted 10 or 20 years ago where things would have reached today, but some businesses have done better than others at riding the wave – and plenty of sophisticated new entrants have emerged to go head-to-head with the established players in a world that not so long ago was characterized by talk of 'clone' high streets and how niche retailers were being crushed by the big players.

That's not today's world – and what has driven the change hasn't so much been the technology as the consumer. Tech has been the great enabler, but it's the multichannel buying habits of consumers that have really changed things. It puts a lot of demands on the retailers, but the benefits are there too for those willing to take a lead with a multichannel proposition that can do more even than the nimble online pure plays.

It's worth staying with this for a moment to ponder the organizational benefits for a multichannel retailer that has fully grasped the opportunity – and comparing it with its bricks-and-mortar incarnation of not so long ago:

- Increased revenue and growth opportunities, with more touch points with consumers.
- Better responsiveness and sensitivity to changing environments.

- Competitive advantage over only pure-plays, particularly around immediacy, education opportunities for complex products and easier returns.
- Organizational efficiency and effectiveness opportunities by sharing processing, technology and information.

And there are customer-related benefits too:

- Better and wider customer interaction, with more information available for improved understanding of customers and identification of opportunities for increasing value per customer.
- Increased customer loyalty through better understanding of those customers and their needs.
- Better customer experience can reduce churn and increase loyalty.
- Great opportunities to improve brand perception.

Of course there are risks and challenges for multichannel retailers too, but our point is that retail offers a vivid demonstration of the need for businesses to keep up with all external developments – or risk being left behind. The decline of Woolworths or HMV or Jessops – or the way Morrisons has been left behind in online supermarket shopping – tell a story that any business in any sector would do well to try to learn from.

Safe as houses?

The need to embrace business agility, and also having that willingness to diversify and disrupt the current business model, is one take-away from all these examples.

In some cases, that kind of change isn't even all that disruptive, either. Consider the world of estate agency for a moment, where the slump in the volume of housing transactions in recent years could have put paid to many of the high-street's estate agents. Most, however, realized that a stagnant house-buying market leads to a stronger rental market, and adjusted the business accordingly. This created new revenues streams by offering rental-related services and also by working hard to understand demographic changes to ensure that the properties being marketed are wanted by the market.

The social network

Of course, some external trends aren't sector specific at all but are near universal – and can change everything.

The rise of social media is one example, having developed quickly at the intersection of the technological and the social. We all understand how it has had a disruptive impact on many businesses, particularly those selling to consumers where reputations can be boosted or undermined online in the blink of an eye.

Arguably it's a change that is felt particularly acutely by those businesses where customer interactions used to happen through call centres – but now those same customers have access to the business through a combination of channels, with social being one of the most widely used options. Consumers can use sites like Facebook and Twitter to follow their favourite brands to stay current with the latest news, take advantage of special promotions and even address service concerns. It's the transparency of social media that has ensured companies are more approachable – which is good for relationship building and customer loyalty for those that get the formula right, and potentially disastrous for those that don't.

We'll add a quick proviso here, however, before moving on: for many small businesses, and particularly those operating in the business-to-business space, we think there's still a danger of becoming distracted by digital communications opportunities at the expense of working at those real, face-to-face relationships with customers. People still buy people, however busy you are in the world of online.

It's something we understand keenly ourselves at Business Doctors, since we know ours is a people business. The business leaders that buy from Business Doctors are buying us as individuals, as well as buying the support we offer. We make sure we never lose sight of that. Email marketing and social media and all the digital options that have emerged to transform many companies' marketing strategies and customer interactions are an important part of the picture of course – but only a part.

Evolution and revolution

We'd like to add to the picture of external opportunities and potential risks now, by emphasizing where this might head.

Here's the point: embarking on this journey is likely to create other spin-off benefits, and that's because today's sophisticated world is set up in particular for sophisticated businesses.

Think about it. The more evolved your business can become, the more opportunities will come its way not just directly but indirectly.

One way to illustrate the point is though the concept of social responsibility.

It's well understood now that being socially responsible is increasingly important for modern organizations – but mainly it is the well-resourced corporates and public sector that pay most attention and take it really seriously; most smaller businesses tend to address CSR only sporadically.

But if CSR is something your business addresses properly, in a rounded way, perhaps as part of a particular agenda in the business to address social issues, there's plenty of evidence of a strong correlation between social performance and financial performance – and think about all those businesses that will be happier to work with demonstrably socially responsible businesses across their supply chain.

The benefits of a rounded CSR policy go far beyond this, however:

- **It reduces risk.** Companies that have made strong efforts to build a good reputation can lose it quickly in the event of a scandal (think Enron) or an accident (e.g. BP's Horizon oil spill). The best way to anticipate and head off such events is to embed social responsibility into organizational culture.
- **It differentiates your product or service.** Companies that want to remain competitive in today's marketplace need to offer differentiated products. It's through product differentiation that you achieve competitive advantage by increasing the perceived value of products relative to the perceived value of the products of competitors. Among SMEs, especially, if you are the one with CSR or the environment on the agenda, that's one way to stand out,

whatever else your product or service looks like. There's plenty of evidence, for example, that firms that offer environmentally friendly products experience higher sales growth than firms that sell conventional products – and usually such products sell at a higher price. Added to this, firms that offer unique value propositions differentiate their products in customers' minds, which builds loyalty based solely on ethical values.

- **It motivates your staff.** Companies that are socially responsible are more likely to recruit and retain the best people. Recent research across six countries (the USA, Brazil, China, India, the UK and Germany) shows that when employees have a positive view of a company's CSR agenda they are more willing to work for it, participate in its efforts, align with its culture and recommend it as the best place to work. Employee satisfaction deriving from corporate social responsibility leads to higher productivity, higher employee retention rate, better overall performance and higher profits.

It's time to get thinking!

Of course CSR is just one simplified example of how your business will benefit from engaging with the big picture, but we think it's a good one. In an era where the protection of the environment is a clear imperative and global warming threatens human existence, social responsibility demonstrates the right values, projects optimism – and puts your business in the right space to work with others that are embracing CSR too. It just makes sense on so many levels – and feeds into many other areas when you start to think about external issues.

The message at its simplest is to understand the big picture, plug yourself in wherever you can – and reap the rewards.

Four steps to future-proof your organization

1. **Start with what's most predictable.** You can track those trends that began in the past, are happening now and are very likely to continue in the future. These kinds of trends often have inbuilt momentum so we can be pretty certain that they will happen.

   Many of these mega-trends – like global population growth, urbanization or climate change – are familiar to most of us. Consider the ones that will have greatest impact and prepare for them.

   For example, on the current trajectory, half of UK shopping will be online in a decade and Amazon will have overtaken Walmart as the biggest retailer in the world. Yet many supermarkets are still building brick and mortar stores.

2. **Think hard about the uncertainties.** How will these mega-trends interact? Are some trends incompatible in the longer term? What will be the political, social and psychological responses?

   A good approach is to develop a set of scenarios for the future. Each will contain elements of what will come to pass, but no single one of them will be entirely correct. Scenarios can help to test today's strategy and to make it more resilient. So, recognizing that there are a range of possible futures, try to think of the best strategy today likely to succeed in all those possible futures.

3. **Scan the horizon for emerging technologies, organizations or patterns of behaviour.** Think of these as the seeds or shoots that are just poking through now, but that will grow into the towering trees and forests of the future. Anything of world-changing importance that will occur over the next 15 to 20 years is already happening somewhere: 'The future is already here, it's just not evenly distributed,' as the writer William Gibson puts it.

4. **The best way to know what the future holds is to create it.** Once you have thought about the future in a structured way, don't be passive in the face of what's to come. Think of ways to make your own luck and create your own future.

Chapter 7

Do you REALLY know your market?

Here's a simple statement to get the chapter under way: your business has opportunities to grow and develop that are **RIGHT THERE ALREADY**, waiting to be taken.

We write this with confidence, because it's true of every functioning business. If you can put aside any preconceptions about your current limitations and what's possible – in other words, what you think you can and can't do – there is **ALWAYS** room for a business to tap opportunity and to grow.

Plenty may tell you otherwise, of course. For example, some of those you work with may be too operationally focused to see beyond the current capabilities of the business to the bigger picture. But we say that you can safely ignore any such wariness. For most businesses the good news is that, at least three-quarters of the time, the avenues to growth don't in fact lie in external opportunities or in developing and achieving a long-term vision that diversifies the proposition. No, they lie a whole lot closer to home than that: in your current known commercial opportunities and in your customers and their needs.

Exploring these opportunities is best done in two stages. First of all you need to put your current set-up under the spotlight, as that will tell you a lot in itself about your customers; after that, you'll do well to focus some attention directly on your customers and what makes them tick.

What is it that we do again?

Many of the best opportunities for a business are easy to see with even some basic analysis. Start at the beginning, then, by looking at the current mix of business across the company. How many different revenue streams are there and how are they best broken down?

These days there are plenty of fancy software dashboards you can use for your analytics, but if that's a bridge too far — and at the outset it probably is — just start with a simple matrix that lists what you do and make, while perhaps also listing market sectors served, your product types and any other meaningful groupings and data clusters.

As you move through an exercise like this, one important area you should start to cover off is the financial side of the equation. What's your turnover and gross profit for each identified area — and your net profit too? If you've not got visibility of any of this, there's a challenge that needs addressing right there. And if you have, you'll quickly know the areas of business that are making money and those that aren't.

Here's a checklist for starters

You'd probably like a few more top-level ideas at this point to get you started, so here's a checklist of areas you might like to explore for your customer-focused market audit:

1. Customers and customer categories

2. Market forces and trends

3. Market segments

4. Products and services

5. Pricing and value

6. The supply chain

7. Competitors

8. The buying process

9. Key drivers affecting demand.

A list like this – and please feel free to work up your own – starts by defining the overall industry sector, its value and current trends. You can then break this down into the market segments most relevant to the business. This would include suppliers, customers, products, competitors, services, strategic partners, market forces and market tends. Finally it's a question of evaluating the buying process and determining the 'critical success factors' (CSFs).

And if you want this process couched in terms of questions rather than headlines, how about this?

1. What market are we in – and how do we define it?

2. How big is the market?

3. Is the market growing, constant or in decline?

4. What's our current share of the cake – how much do we need to succeed?

5. Where are the opportunities for growth?

6. Who are our most valuable customers?

7. How, why and when do they buy?

8. What is our share of their spend?

9. Do they buy across the full range of our products and services?

10. Do they buy from our competitors?

11. Why do they spend with our competitors?

12. How much more could they spend with us?

13. Can we sell to different market segments?

14. What is critical to our success in this market?

Nice (and nasty) surprises

If that's a useful starting point for this exercise, it's also time for a word of caution.

We find all too often when working with companies that many aren't good enough at apportioning their centralized costs. Frankly this is a big problem: knowing precisely what goes where in financial terms is something you need to get to grips with – and fast.

Also, once you dive in you'll doubtless find some nice and some nasty surprises through this kind of analysis. Just as you might find some elements of the business that haven't even had much attention are performing surprisingly well as a profit centre, far too often that will be counterbalanced by the shock that some long-standing or core elements of the business are not improving the bottom line. The challenge then is to see whether that's something that can be turned around with some changes – or whether the focus of operations in fact needs to go elsewhere.

It's not about the top line

Our fundamental point, of course, is that generating revenues is never enough in itself in business – you need to be making profits. It's natural, if the going gets tough, to think that taking on less profitable business that keeps everyone busy is a good way to weather the storm. But that's really not a good game to play – all too easily, you will be weighed down by parts of the business that are growing the company's losses rather than growing profits.

Made to measure

Knowing what your customer values when they buy from you is important for any business to understand.

One company I worked with recently was a long-established manufacturer and servicer of precision measuring equipment that's used in advanced manufacturing.

The company is based in the UK but operates in an international market, with competition from China and elsewhere.

At the point where I started to work with it, the company had suffered several challenging trading years, characterized by growing overseas competition that had driven down prices and changed the dynamics of the marketplace.

The company was committed to UK production using high quality materials but the growth of competition from overseas, using different materials and producing certified measuring equipment that was adequate and compliant without being exceptional, had put real pressure on the business. It had effectively put a cap on the price of its UK-produced product which meant it was making its core product at a loss.

The good news, though, was that the company's malaise could be overcome.

Once I started to talk to its customers, it became clear that what they valued in the business was its heritage and brand name and its ability to sell certified products, as much as the high quality of its own equipment. That meant the company had an absolute advantage in the market, whether or not it was producing and selling the highest-quality precision equipment on which it prided itself.

This realization – gleaned by starting conversations with its customers and nothing more – changed everything. It meant the company could start to sell on certified equipment made by third parties – and make a profit on every sale. And it meant it could still fulfil UK orders for a small, dedicated niche of companies that were willing to pay a premium for the very best UK product.

What had been a situation that briefly looked insurmountable was soon turned into an opportunity to put the company back on a comfortably profitable footing – and with a business model that in many ways was less challenging and challenged all round.

Some might instinctively argue that the company's values and commitment to high standards were compromised when it repositioned its offer, but the basic commitment to high quality was still there, and the company was transparent to all its customers about the changes it made. So what's a better tactic? Uphold certain values that will drive you out of business – or change tack, tell everyone what you are doing and why, and get back to a profitable trading position?

I know where I stand in relation to that particular conundrum. A company with the 'right' values but no business to speak of really can't be said to be doing the right thing, by any useful measure.

Rod

Removing risk

The principle behind trying to understand your best customers and your best opportunities for profitable business is a simple one: to find the least-risky way to grow the business and its bottom line.

There's a time-honoured way to start with this sort of approach and that's to look for what every jargon-spouting consultant nowadays calls the 'easy wins'.

It's a fair enough phrase really, even if starts to grate when you've heard it a thousand times. And for companies that specialize in business-to-business over business-to-consumer markets, the good news is that any search for those quick wins can often be achieved relatively easily.

That's because for many B2B-focused businesses with a turn-over of between £1 m and £20 m, where we do most of our work, it's usually straightforward to identify which customers to try to understand better – you start with the biggest! In all likelihood your top 5 or 10 (or sometimes 15 or 20) customers will account for a huge slice of your overall business – more than three-quarters, we are willing to bet – so understanding their needs, how you serve them currently and where you could do more, represents a huge step forward.

Customers, customer types and supply chains

This list of key customers is great to have, but it's only a beginning. Before you can think about approaching them in fact-finding mode, to glean more insights, you need to ensure you understand them – and more specifically their relationship with you.

There's lots you can do here, but a good place to start is to try mapping your different customer types and, through that, how and why they buy from you. At the same time, you can also map all your other business relationships as part of the exercise. What companies are in your supply chain and why do you buy from them? Are any of these groups also customers of yours?

Sometimes there is a lot of complexity to explore around this. Consider a specialist glass and window manufacturer we worked with: it had clients in the public sector like local councils, placing order for projects from council offices to schools to libraries; plus private sector clients from a range of contexts – offices, shopping centres and leisure facilities, but also from different parts of the supply chain too, from construction companies to architectural metalworkers and more.

In fact, understanding how the supply chains that touch you all fit together is an important step. Who buys from whom – and why? Are the dynamics of the supply chain – everyone you buy from and sell to, and the companies that they in turn trade with – really changing? In some sectors, like aerospace and automotive, the global car- and plane-makers increasingly want a simpler supply chain, which means more assembly work taking place through a shrinking pool of subcontractors. And most supply chains are dynamic and shifting to some extent, remember. Any company that doesn't understand where it fits into a supply chain that's changing is vulnerable to this change: the risk is that it won't be managing its relationships and changing its business model in a proactive way that helps it to remain relevant to all its partners.

Good to great: the difference customer insight can make

Consider this consumer scenario.

I shop at two grocery stores. I am a regular customer, stopping by at least once if not twice a week. Nearly every time I'm at the checkout, I end up having a conversation with the person on the till. It's nice to be able to do that, since they're both small operations and the customer flow is steady but not manic.

In Store A the till operators are friendly. As they ring me up, we might chat for a moment about the weather or something from the morning newspaper. All very pleasant. The next time I go in, they're just as hospitable, but there's no hint of recognition of me as a regular shopper. It's as if they've never seen me before.

As I approach the cash register at Store B, the till operator asks me how I liked those fancy tea bags I bought last week, or how my wife liked the smell of that hand cream they saw me trying out. They'll remember the special diet I'm on and recommend a product that just arrived in the store. They, too, give me samples and tell me to have a nice day, but this time when I leave, I feel they just might ask me how that day went the next time they see me.

Store A has good customer service, something that's acceptable to most business owners. Nice, helpful employees that toe the party line. No fuss, no muss.

Store B has outstanding customer service. They're delivering a great shopping experience, subtly working to give shoppers more than they expected. And they're genuinely interested in their customers as individuals.

> *Guess which store is opening in new locations to meet customer demand?*
>
> *It doesn't take the memory of an elephant to remember your customers or clients, just a little more awareness of the universe around you – and your patrons. That's why getting to know your customers matters.*
>
> **Matt**

First, second and third tier customers

Once you've mapped some of the complexity in your supply chain, and thought about your individual customer relationships, the natural next step is to try to categorize your customers in terms of their importance to you.

It's not just the type of business you do with them that counts, but all the important variables you can muster. How much business do they do with you? Is it the right kind of business from your perspective? How strong is the relationship between you and them? What is the basis for that relationship and who manages it? What are the profit margins on the business that you do? Could the customer be buying the same product or service elsewhere – and what would it be costing?

One big objective here is to be able to identify which customers are most important you – your first-tier customers – plus your second- and third-tier customers in terms of their significance.

Understand, though, that all of these tiers of customers matter and are crucial to the success of your company, even though you have categorized their relative significance.

If you want to really grasp this point, think of the way an airline fills an aeroplane. It has business-class passengers, premium economy passengers and economy passengers on its flights – and all are important to making that flight commercially viable. The plane won't fly without any particular group. Your business works the same.

You can take the analogy further too. Some of your customers probably look a lot like the airline's economy passengers – they've screwed you down on price but the business is still worth having – some will look like premium economy and the most profitable, tier-one, customers will look like the airline's business-class passengers.

But we also know the picture isn't complete yet. Just as an airline will have some business-class passengers that have never booked before and about whom it knows almost nothing, while others are frequent flyers that it knows a lot about, your knowledge about your customers is also inconsistent – and the best way to fill in the blanks is to start talking to them.

Finding out more: four more approaches to knowing your customer

1. **Try to think like them.** Put yourself in your customers' shoes and imagine how they live their lives. Think about every detail. This will help you speak to them better, because it enables you to know what they want. In order to do this, you have to know your target customer, so that's step one before you embark on this.

2. **Read your competitors' sales pitches.** One good way to determine your customers' problems is to read the sales letters of others. Notice what benefits they are emphasizing. If lots of the marketing makes the same points then it's probably important. The next step is to work out how to deliver a better answer than anyone else.

3. **Carry out an easy, conversational survey.** It's simple but it usually works. Not a full-on piece of market research but a chatty survey that asks your customers what their main problems are in a more conversational way. With online resources like Survey Monkey now available, this approach has never been easier to deliver.

4. **Visit online forums.** In forums you should find the main problems people are talking about. It will also help you to know what to focus on with your product. If you see certain questions coming up again and again, you know this is something you want to emphasize.

Start that customer conversation

It's highly probable that there are things you'd like to know about every one of your customers. Could you say hand on heart that you have a perfect view of any single customer and understand perfectly how and why it buys from you – and that the relationship you have with it could not be optimized or improved in any way? Of course you couldn't.

So that's the starting point: for each of your newly segmented most-valuable customers the idea is to find out more and to develop the relationship as far as you can take it.

Perhaps the crucial point to make here is this: we think this should be a process that you conduct on a **CASE BY CASE** basis, rather than undertaking a standard survey of any kind. Getting to understand your best customers like this is an exercise in market penetration above all else – selling smarter and selling more to those you know best of all. There is plenty of theory out there about how to conduct an effective survey of your customers and markets, but what we are pushing for here is more conversations and specific questions to augment what you know already.

The questions that you are looking to answer may look a bit like this:

1. How, why and when does the customer spend with us?
2. What is our share of this spend?
3. Do they buy across the full range of our products and services?
4. Do they buy from our competitors?
5. Why do they spend with our competitors?
6. How much more could they spend with us?

Just how you go about getting good answers will vary a lot, however. With some, there will be a strong personal relationship in place between a key individual or individuals in your business and key individuals in theirs. It might just be a question of proposing a meeting, being transparent about why you are asking for it, and booking it in.

With others, the challenge may be more complex. Do you have those strong relationships into the business? Do you know enough about how and why they buy from you – or is the relationship quite a distant one? Have there ever been any issues or disputes in the past that need to be acknowledged or that have complicated relations? Is the company buying less from you than previously – and do you know the reason why?

You will know – or can find out – the particular dynamics in relation to the key customers for your business. You'll need to just get stuck in and come up with the right plans, perhaps proceeding two (or one or three or four) customers at a time with the programme and reviewing progress as you go. What insights are coming out along the way? Is the process looking like it will lead to stronger relationships and new business quickly, or will it take time to develop things further?

There's one more point to make before we close this chapter. Although a targeted approach is what's needed for those individual customer insights, many of the learnings that start to come out of the process will have a far wider application.

Imagine if you start to discover, over the course of many conversations with different customers, that many aren't as price-sensitive as you suspected they were in relation to certain products and services you offer? Or that a slightly tweaked version of the product or service would be something the customer would happily pay extra for? Being offered up this kind of insight direct from a customer is not as silly as it might sound to you. In fact, many will be happy to tell you the difference a product or service makes to them, and if it turns out that benefit far outweighs the cost then that's usually something your partners and customers are happy to share. You are part of what makes their business successful and profitable, and most will be delighted to explore it further.

Just get started

Before we sign off this chapter there is a point worth drawing out here. Getting to **REALLY** know your customers is something that can have an almost immediate transformative impact on your business. Many of the other ideas and approaches we cover in these pages are longer-term strategies and plans to get your business on track, even if the implementation can kick off very quickly. But with the work you put into your customers there's every chance you'll get some payback very quickly – and it might even feel like a game-changer in its own right.

So if you feel like pursuing an instant fix alongside your other work on the business, this a great place to focus your energies.

Ten things you should know about your customers

1. **Who they are.** If you sell to individuals, find out your customers' gender, age, marital status, job – and so on. If you sell to other businesses, find out what size and kind of business they are.

2. **What they do.** If you sell directly to individuals, it's worth knowing their occupations and interests. If you sell to other businesses, it helps to have an understanding of what their business is trying to achieve.

3. **Why they buy.** If you know why customers buy a product or service, it's easier to match their needs to the benefits your business can offer.

4. **When they buy.** If you approach a customer just at the time they want to buy, you will massively increase your chances of success.

5. **How they buy.** For example, some people prefer to buy from a website, while others prefer a face-to-face meeting.

6. **How much money they have.** You'll be more successful if you can match what you're offering to what you know your customer can afford.

7. **What makes them feel good about buying.** If you know what makes them tick, you can serve them in the way they prefer.

8. **What they expect of you.** For example, if your customers expect reliable delivery and you don't disappoint them, you stand to gain repeat business.

9. **What they think about you.** If your customers enjoy dealing with you, they're likely to buy more. And you can only tackle problems that customers have if you know what they are.

10. **What they think about the competition.** If you know how your customers view the competition, you stand a better chance of staying ahead of them it.

Chapter 8

Are you ready to look in the mirror?

The outward-looking process of trying to understand your customer and your market opportunities better, as outlined in Chapters 6 and 7, will undoubtedly reveal where you can win new business and evolve the company across the board.

This chapter offers another take on the theme of opportunity (and of risk) by asking you to turn the spotlight firmly back on the business. The challenge here is to work out where best to focus your energies and attention for success – and what needs to be addressed for problems to be avoided.

Call it a sanity check. It's necessary because an exciting list of partially understood – even if quite detailed – opportunities is one thing, but really feeling confident that you know where to start, and why, is something else. Which of the apparent opportunities are real and convertible, and which would demand a lot of time and effort – and then still end up being risky?

With these sorts of questions in mind, we've developed a methodology for approaching the challenge that we've found to work exceptionally well when applied.

What's GIVE?

Like many good methodologies, ours is captured in an acronym: GIVE arises from the headline ideas of Great, Improve, Vulnerable and Edge.

You could probably guess how the keywords apply, but we'll save you the bother. Try these:

- Where are we GREAT?
- Where can we IMPROVE?
- Where are we VULNERABLE?
- Where is our business EDGE?

These four headline questions are aimed squarely at unlocking the reality of your current capabilities and opportunities as a business. Answered constructively and systematically, they will give you an understanding of how you can achieve maximum growth with the least risk.

Before we explore further, it's worth saying a few brief words about the use of GIVE as a methodology in a world where there are plenty of other well-known evaluation tools being used. You've probably heard of the SWOT matrix, for example, which structures business planning around a consideration of Strengths, Weaknesses, Opportunities and Threats.

Well, we think SWOT and some other methodologies are useful for this sort of exercise, but in the context of this book GIVE is preferable because of its strong focus on the positive development of the business and the way it builds on the other work contained in these pages. In other words, GIVE has been developed specifically to plug into our overall approach to doing better business.

More than self-analysis

As we start to explore this approach, one more thing to say is that the use of GIVE should be about more than board-room self-analysis. In fact, this is an opportunity for the board to involve other stakeholders, from workers to shareholders, strategic partners to suppliers. Gathering together inputs from everyone that's engaged with the business and its performance should be an effort that repays itself with a more rounded understanding of all the business's capabilities and vulnerabilities.

But let's stop the preamble there: what does G stand for again?

G is for GREAT!

The factors that help to make a business great will vary wildly from one company to the next – and that can make the challenge of identifying your company's particular X-factor a harder job than it might at first sound.

Perhaps you've got a great brand name that sets you apart from the competition. Something that's widely known, easily remembered and with a strong reputation in the marketplace.

Or maybe, and less obviously, it's your business relationships that help the company to stand apart. You might be a business that's plugged into a sophisticated supply chain in a way that makes you an important player for those upstream and downstream of your products and services.

Equally it might be something as prosaic as where you are based that holds the key to the company's greatness. Perhaps you've a huge number of customers and suppliers within two hours' travel time, and can access places, and hence business opportunities, in a way that is enabling the company to be responsive when it needs to be. And maybe your access is that much better than that enjoyed by the main competition, exaggerating the advantage you have.

Or, again, perhaps it's the intellectual property in the business that sets it apart: you've developed a unique product that's better than the alternatives in its marketplace and which is protected so it cannot be easily replicated or copied.

To these notional descriptions we could add several hundred others that would resonate strongly with someone out there. The point we are emphasizing is that what you think makes the company great and what actually sets it apart may not be quite the same thing. Just because the company's success came one way at one point in its history doesn't mean that the particular advantage it enjoyed then is what makes it great today. As the previous chapters have explored, the world out there is constantly changing, as are the requirements of your customers, so it would be unusual, not to say strange, if the company's story – its greatness – remained the same in the face of such change.

You should expect this exploration of just what makes the company great to have other benefits, too. A review process like this will peel away some of your misguided preconceptions about the business to reveal opportunity, but it should also help you to see how the business can be better organized – and why some of the opportunities identified were missed in the first place.

As companies grow they are reorganized again and again – sometimes week to week, more commonly month to month

— and often in haphazard ways. A look at what's great in today's context is therefore also a chance to take a step back from the business to look at it anew:

- Are some parts of the business isolated from other parts?

- Are the connections across the business as strong as they need to be for information to flow where it needs to in order for the right decisions to be reached?

- Is the business being held back because there aren't the necessary skills to make certain things happen?

- Or are some products or services not pulling their weight and acting as a drain on activity and profitability elsewhere?

I is for IMPROVE!

Which bring us onto the next question you should be asking: where can we IMPROVE?

Nearly everything in life and in business can be improved, can't it? Your company is no different. In fact, we could make a case that the longer the list of potential improvements you can muster the better. It means there is more for you to go at as you look to make a better business.

At the same time, you also need to be quite systematic here. A long, unfocused list of the 'improvable' won't help you. What you need to do is to narrow it down to the key parts of the business and come up with some specifics: think about things like job roles, accountability, reporting lines, customer service and any other important elements or functions that you need to consider.

One thing that will very likely need to be improved, as we've touched on in earlier chapters, is your company's management of its financial information, as this is something that underpins many of the other decisions you need to take as a business.

Why do we say this? Simply because if you don't know your costs and profit margins on particular products and services, and if you aren't on top of your financial planning and sales planning and key account management at every step, then the risk is that the business doesn't have the foundations it needs to be successful. (This is something we look at again in the book's final chapter.)

So a focus on the financial foundations is one priority, but there is another area of almost equal importance here.

Experience tells us that somewhere high on this list of areas to improve will be marketing.

Why? Because we find again and again, after some soul-searching, that marketing and communications is a crucial area that many small businesses need to improve.

Most small businesses struggle with effective marketing simply because they don't have the internal expertise and resources to do it well enough. There's no shame in understanding this – quite the opposite, in fact – since marketing has been changing more rapidly than ever before in this digital age. Online engagement is something that's particularly hard to grasp for many business-to-business operations that, until recently, may have relied on a basic, contact-us website, some print brochures, a small sales team out in the field – and little else.

In 2014, most are beginning to understand that that's not enough. The typical SME, with a brochure site that doesn't relate to customers and would-be customers and that makes no attempt to pull in new enquiries and convert them into customers, is treading on thin ice.

Our point here is that improvement is so much more than a nice-to-have: a transformation is very likely what's needed because many businesses will be losing far more customer leads than they win when visitors arrive at their website and ponder whether to follow through. Content is king for today's businesses in marketing terms, and companies that aren't delivering something immediately reassuring, interesting and eye-catching to would-be customers – something that grabs someone's attention and keeps it – are likely to hit trouble sooner rather than later.

V is for VULNERABLE!

The question of where a business is vulnerable could be taken as offering another perspective on where a business might improve. But when considering business vulnerability, it's the particular angle you take that counts.

In Chapter 6 you'll remember we introduced the idea of a PEST analysis – looking at political, economic, social and technological issues – to future-proof against the shifting landscape inhabited by the business.

Well, this time around the question of where the business is VULNERABLE should focus on the immediate picture – areas where the business might improve, yes, but also just a chance to take stock of the here and now to avoid having any illusions.

Here are some questions you might need to ask:

1. Which of our products and services could realistically be bought by our customers elsewhere?
2. Are we in a position to compete in all the markets where we are active?
3. Is our current pricing being led by the dynamics in today's marketplace or is it informed by some historical practices?
4. Are we adding value for our customers that isn't being reflected in the prices that we are charging?
5. If we increased our prices, how many customers might realistically want to look elsewhere? (And would price alone be enough for them to jump without even a backwards glance?)
6. Are we too reliant on a handful of customers in some of our markets?

There is plenty of overlap between these questions, of course, but that final question – essentially, do we have too few customers for service x or product y? – often looms largest among the issues those and other similar questions might table.

It's an obvious point, but almost nothing makes a company more vulnerable than being overly reliant on just a handful of customers. Worse than that, it's very often the case that a company will have just ONE customer that accounts for a big slice of business in a particular market. There can be real day-to-day advantages to having a handful of established customers whose needs your business knows in detail and can serve (and even anticipate). But you ignore the vulnerability that goes hand in hand with that convenience at your peril.

How much of your turnover for a key product or service does your number one customer account for? What about the top three or top five? What's the nature of the relationship you have with these key customers? How confident can you be, realistically, that they won't or can't take their business elsewhere?

If what you find as you start to explore this are some facts that make you feel even remotely uncomfortable then you should take things a lot further. You'll probably want to embrace a detailed and systematic review of your customer mix and customer relationships for the products and services where you feel vulnerable, and in parallel undertake some work on where and how new customers can be secured.

That's just a beginning, of course, and one approach among many we might have highlighted, but we hope it's got you thinking.

E is for EDGE!

What gives your company an edge? What helps to differentiate it from others to give you unique advantages?

We aren't simply asking you here to repeat the big things that help to make your business GREAT, but want you to identify all the details in the business – many of them quite small – that go towards giving you an edge in your markets.

Some of these elements might have to do with clear internal capabilities and efficiencies that you've evolved over time that no competitor could easily replicate. It might have to do with all the invaluable experience and insight and market knowledge you carry within your teams. Or it could be a strategic partnership you've fostered over some years that is helping the business already and holds the potential to do more or open up new revenue streams.

Equally there might be an external factor that's playing into your hands and giving you an advantage over the competition: for a property-industry company, say, there might be a tram-line that's opening up on your patch that will boost conditions locally, playing into your hands in a market where you are already well-established.

Just as when seeking out what makes a company GREAT, however, not everything that gives you an EDGE will be immediately obvious — or half-ignored, at any rate. Here are two contrasting examples to illustrate the point.

EDGE example 1: The construction company

We worked with a construction company with a different mentality to much of the competition — but one that the owner wasn't using to his advantage. He was engaging with us on a range of issues, but what jumped out immediately was the point that this was a company that got the job done — and quickly. The company records showed job after job being completed on or ahead of schedule because that was how the owner liked to organize things: take a job on, deliver it to a realistic timetable, move on to the next assignment. It was just how he and the business operated, backed up by a network of efficient, effective subcontractors.

This way of working is just not the norm in an industry where many construction companies take on work to schedules they simply won't be able to deliver, for a variety of reasons. Most customers understand and expect that, too, and build in contingency for schedules that slip and costs that climb, maybe with some penalties built in should things go badly wrong.

This ability to set a timetable and stick to it – embedded right across the business – gave the company a real competitive EDGE, of course. And we could see how it gave them a service that plenty of customers would be very happy to pay for.

With this in mind we rebranded the business to make a virtue of this deadline-hitting capability by making it a service offer, with a premium price-tag attached. Overnight it became a 'fast-track' construction company with a rare market offer: to hit deadlines and to commit to hitting them in the contract – and with a track record of doing so – instilling confidence all round.

This repositioning has been a huge success because the market opportunity was always there. It is hugely valuable to many leisure and retail businesses in particular to know that a building will be ready to open its doors on a given date. It means they can take forward bookings with confidence and take full advantage of seasonal spikes in demand. Paying extra for this certainty simply makes perfect sense because the assurance means a company can start meaningful trading many weeks or months sooner than it would otherwise.

EDGE example 2: The stem cell collection business

Stem cell collection is a service to collect umbilical-cord-blood stem cells from a baby the moment it is born, with the aim of taking advantage of current and future opportunities arising from the use of stem cells in a broad range of 'regenerative' medical treatments.

It's a niche market but an international one. In the UK it's dominated by some big players, such as Virgin Health Bank (VH, part of the Virgin group of companies fronted by Richard Branson).

We worked with a client that was active in this space but new to the market and struggling to make inroads against its bigger competition. These competitors, including VHB, mainly operate online, picking up leads using pay-per-click advertising and then sending out a medical pack to those buying the service, to enable stem cell collection by a cooperative midwife.

Our client's offer was the same but different, in that it wasn't able to offer national coverage but used a base in Lincolnshire. And here, once we started to look, was where we found its EDGE.

The self-service element of stem cell collection is what makes the offer scalable for larger business, but it's also a potential weakness. We could see that our Lincolnshire business could not compete on the same terms as its national competition, but could offer something distinct to the parents involved in the 60,000 or so births seen in the area each year.

A local clinic, engagement with local midwives to boost stem cell collection rates, and that face-to-face opportunity to talk it through with parents and parents-in-waiting all added up to something different and distinct from the national competition. We rebranded the business with a less abstract name, opened local clinics, encouraged the forging of local relationships – and the company was away. It could still use pay-per-click advertising, too, but geographically focused for the area it served. It soon proved itself a strong, distinctive offer in the market — making use of its locally focused EDGE that up until then the owner had only perceived as a weakness ('I can't deliver national coverage').

S is for SO WHAT?

Sometimes when we embark on this exercise with business owners there's an extra letter in our acronym, and GIVE becomes GIVES.

The 'S' is short for SO WHAT? — and we like to ask this question as a reminder to sense-check the strategy that is starting to take shape.

Do your plans stand up to scrutiny? If strategy is simply an effort to match market opportunity with internal capability to find your company's **sustainable competitive advantage**, do the ideas and opportunities and differentiators you've come up with work in the real world, or did you go off course along the way?

One useful way of testing your thinking is to ask yourself these critically minded questions:

- What makes my company different?
- What will make my company better?
- What do we want our customers to think?
- What do we want our customers to do?

If everything you've pulled together feels like it is helping you answer these questions usefully and in detail, you are surely on the right track — and the next chapter awaits you.

Seven ways to gain a competitive advantage

1. **Analyze your target market and identify your competition.** Your target market is a specific group of customers at which you aim your products and services. To uncover this market, try these questions: What am I selling? Who will most likely buy or consume my product or service? Also find out which businesses are going after your same target market. How do they differentiate themselves from other companies in the industry? Where are they located?

2. **Learn from your competition.** Don't be afraid of your competition, but rather use it as a learning tool and assess their business model. Learn your competitors' strengths and weaknesses, and then imitate their strengths and use their weaknesses to your advantage. The business information you learn from your rivals will help you develop the competitive edge you need to surpass them in your industry.

3. **Listen to your customers and think like them.** Listening to customers is one of the strategies that will give you a competitive edge. Survey them briefly, encourage feedback – good and bad – at every opportunity. These small insights can make a world of difference. The other thing to do is to start thinking like your customers. Every time you do something that affects them, ask: how would I feel about that? Being customer-centric rather than product- or service-centric is critical.

4. **Create a barrier to entry.** Take advantage of barriers to entry into the market, using them to dissuade competitors from challenging your market share. In some

cases, an established company's ability to manipulate hurdles to enter and compete in its market becomes an effective tool against new competition, further entrenching the business and preserving its profit potential for the future.

5. **Keep innovating.** Once you've gained a competitive advantage, your work continues. To be successful, you will need to maintain your competitive advantage. After all, your competitors are not going to sit back and allow you to steal their market share. You can maintain your competitive advantage by predicting future trends in your industry, constantly researching and monitoring your competitors, and adapting to your customer's wants and needs. Sometimes you may need to take chances to keep ahead of the pack and differentiate your business, but with big risk often comes big reward.

6. **Use the data.** The information revolution is here – don't ignore it! It creates a competitive advantage by providing companies with new ways to outperform their rivals. Knowledge is power, and business information is out there waiting to be analyzed.

7. **Tell your full story.** People buy off those they know, like and trust. How can would-be customers get to know you if all you have on your website is the same old company spiel? Set out a real, transparent vision about your business and your customers, because your potential customers are making decisions about whether or not to contact you every day. If they have the whole story they can make a decision based on what and who you really are.

Part Three

THE WOW FACTOR

*The way that companies reach their customers, and the way they deliver for them, is changing. In today's transparent business world it's not enough to be run-of-the-mill – delivering a wow factor in just the right way for every one of your customers is what's needed. It's this concept that Part Three of the book explores, with the aim of sharpening your focus and getting you thinking about your business through the eyes of your customers. First, in Chapter 9, we'll have you concentrating on those things you really **CAN** emphasize to stand out from the crowd. Then, in Chapter 10, we will have you focused on, and properly understanding, all the benefits that flow from having a really well-targeted customer offer.*

Chapter 9

Are you ready to stand out from the crowd?

Chapter 8 put the focus back on the business, and specifically looked at how to address all the opportunities and risks that attach to it.

For Chapters 9 and 10, the idea is to sharpen that focus and get you thinking about your business **THROUGH THE EYES OF YOUR CUSTOMERS**.

The rationale here is simple. Some of the things that make your business special aren't for sharing with the world: this is the SO WHAT? bit in the GIVES acronym we talked about right at the end of Chapter 8. If, say, your location gives you an advantage over the competition, that's great news but it's surely not something to brag about.

In this chapter, we want you concentrating on those things you really **CAN** emphasize to stand out from the crowd. These are the stories about the business that resonate with customers and matter to them. What's more, there's little chance of them eliciting a 'so what?' response from anyone, because what you are saying goes to the heart of your customer offer.

To get you started, use the questions from Chapter 8 to set the scene again:

- What makes my company different?
- What will make my company better?
- What do we want our customers to think?
- What do we want our customers to do?

The aim of these questions should be obvious: you need a clear understanding of the customer offer you are putting out there, of how and why you are trying to develop the business for your customers – and you need a grip on your customer relationships too.

What's our offer again?

If a company isn't offering something distinctive in its marketplace then there is not much reason to have confidence that it will grow.

It is just about possible that some businesses without a distinctive offer could still pick up work based on a territorial advantage (particularly, say, if they are the sole supplier of an especially immobile product). Or others with a run-of-the-mill offer that are facing up to competitors might be able to drive business by being competitive on price in some contexts.

But neither of these scenarios gives much cause for optimism about the long term – particularly when you consider that smaller businesses don't usually have the critical mass to generate the economies of scale that can generate a real price advantage. For the country's small and medium-sized businesses, in fact, what usually sets them apart from the competition is rooted in a specific service offer that precisely meets the needs of a particular client group or groups.

So the question is this: are you confident that you know what your particular point of difference or distinction is, and why your customers love you?

A winning difference

This point about differentiation should really give pause for thought – and is worth exploration.

Companies get paid not just for performing a valuable task but for being different from their competitors in a manner that lets them boost profits for their core customers.

Usually, too, it also holds that the sharper that point of differentiation, the greater the advantage. To illustrate this, let's briefly think big and consider Tetra Pak, a company that in 2010 sold more than 150 billion packages in 170 markets around the world. Tetra Pak's carton packages extend the shelf life of products and often cut the need for refrigeration. The shapes they take – squares and pyramids in the main – stack more efficiently in trucks and on shelves than most cans or bottles. And the packaging machines that use the company's unique laminated material lend themselves to high-volume dairy operations. These few features set Tetra Pak well apart from many competitors and allow it to produce a package that more than compensates for its cost.

In fact, any analysis of companies that manage to sustain a high level of performance over many years invariably shows that more than three-quarters of them have this kind of well-defined and easily understood differentiation to fall back on. Sometimes it's a story they can take to their customers too (as in Tetra Pak's case) but not always.

In the consumer space, things very often get complicated when it comes to the stories worth telling customers. Among the big brands, we can say that Nike's differentiation resides in the power of its brand, in the company's relationships with top athletes, and in its signature performance-focused product design – but the marketing message to consumers is mostly focused elsewhere, emphasizing a brand value ('just do it') and a style above all else.

At Apple, meanwhile, the company's differentiation lies in its ability to keep creating easy-to-use software and hardware that adds to its existing software-and-hardware ecosystem, built around a relatively simple (though high-margin and high-value) design and product line with just a few dozen core products. Again, though, that's not the message to customers, many of whom are successfully encouraged to be devoted and to see all things Apple as signifying class, taste and cool.

Over the long run, however, what sets Apple and other market leaders apart has everything to do with a company's strategic differentiation and execution. Every industry has leaders and laggards, and the leaders are the most highly differentiated.

Something else that's worth noting, before we turn back to the question of your point of difference in the eyes of customers, is that differentiation is also hard to sustain – and not just because competitors try hard to undermine or replicate it. Often the big problem is internal: the growth generated by successful differentiation begets complexity, and a complex company risks ignoring what it's good at. Hence Apple trying to keep its product lines simple as far as it possibly can, and being as consistent as possible in all that it does, from products to store designs to customer service to high-end pricing.

Consistently successful companies are, in short, working hard at not having to reinvent themselves through periodic 'binge and purge' strategies. Instead they relentlessly build on their fundamental differentiation, going from strength to strength. They learn to deliver their differentiation to the front line, creating an organization that lives and breathes its strategic advantages day in and day out. And they learn how to sustain this over time through constant adaptation to changes in the market.

The result is a simple, repeatable business model that a company can apply to new products and markets over and over again to generate sustained growth.

What's the WRONG story to tell?

With that small detour into the importance of business differentiation behind us, let's now return to the idea of getting a story together that's just right for your customers.

So what **DON'T** customers care about?

- Customers probably don't care if you are the number one provider in your market.
- They probably don't care that you give more money to charity than a rival.
- They may well not care that you are a family business (though in some contexts they just might).
- Customers probably aren't interested in **ANY** story that sounds smug and self-congratulatory and not about their needs.

So what's the RIGHT story?

For so many small businesses, the difference lies in the detail of the offer to the customer, and that's what needs to be sold.

Here's a first-hand example from the highly competitive, commoditized world of logistics. When it comes to delivering any goods the primary function is of course to get a package from point A to point B undamaged and on time – if you can do that, you are in the game. But it also means the point of differentiation for logistics firms normally lies elsewhere – and particularly in customer service.

One of our Business Doctors clients in this market space has carved out its niche offering outsourced logistics to small businesses. Its sweet spot is not efficient and timely package delivery – that's a given – but lies in servicing the needs of customers that do not have a dedicated internal logistics resource but are prepared to pay a premium for another company to take the strain. In other words our client is effectively an intermediary – but an approachable one in a market populated largely by giant corporates offering automated, faceless customer service. The point of differentiation is, then, the human scale of the business and the way it interacts with its customers. Whatever else is happening in the world, its customers know they won't have to deal with website logins and giant call centres every step of the way, but instead can pick up the phone and talk to someone plugged in and knowledgeable to get things done. We probably don't need to say much more to convince you what value lies in that.

Lighting up more than Christmas

Some companies start off in a clever niche, so differentiation is already part of the business DNA, but even businesses like these have to reinvent themselves along the way, to cope with competition and to take advantage of growth opportunities.

One company Business Doctors has worked with over many years is a provider of professional-standard low-energy Christmas lights and decorations. In the main it sells to the retail and leisure sector, as well as doing a small amount of business with corporates in other sectors and with wealthy private individuals.

Today the company's core business, installing and running the Christmas decorations and lights for shopping centres and retail chains, is strong in the face of a certain amount of specialist competition, but the company is now pushing into distinct new markets, trading on its sourcing and detailed understanding of low-energy products.

This push has been partly driven by the seasonal nature of its core business, which means it could have untapped capacity for much of the year, but is also a reflection of the expertise and understanding the business has built up over a long period.

The point is, this would be an easy expertise for the company to have overlooked. Its core business is commercially successful, which would be enough for some boardrooms. Yet the directors have always put a priority on developing existing relationships with each of its customers when it could easily have opted for an arm's-length, transaction-driven approach based around the Christmas lights and nothing more. By working hard at fostering relationships and regular conversations it has managed to trade on its low-energy lighting expertise and its energy-efficiency know-how very success-fully. These are useful services to many retailers facing up to high and rising energy costs, so it was just a question of chipping away at the opportunity however it could.

Recently the business has also started to scale this new business in a risk-free way by packaging up what and who it knows as a franchise opportunity. (This is often a particularly good option for businesses that have created business systems and relationships that aren't easily replicable, as in this case.)

All in all, the company's approach offers one good example of the importance of learning from customers and keeping on diversifying to take the business in new directions.

Please those customers!

Differentiation is about understanding where you fit best and can deliver the most value – and that will often mean building on features that deviate from the average characteristics of your industry. By focusing on those features that achieve what your customers want, you'll give buyers a reason to choose your brand (your product, your service) over others. And by increasing the differentiated value of your product or service to customers, you'll have a better chance of boosting your margins and of the competition struggling to copy you.

So, if you haven't really pushed it yet, this is the moment to think creatively and laterally – 'outside of the box' if you will. How can you go against the norm and adopt a bold approach to doing business in your industry? You should be looking to focus on those aspects of the business that you believe you can uniquely excel at. Here are some examples of values and benefits you might want to explore:

- Superior service
- Greater product availability
- Higher quality
- Better performance
- Better intelligence
- Greater durability
- A respected image
- Technology leadership
- A satisfaction guarantee
- Faster delivery
- More customer support.

Remember, too, that whatever you choose to emphasize and embark on today is only a beginning: differentiating your business offer to customers is an ongoing process because the marketplace is always changing. You need to be prepared to keep changing with it – but also to keep doing it in your own unique way.

DANGER! You can't please everyone

Why is a targeted offer so important? Just consider what happens when you try to be all things to all customers.

We worked with one financial advisory business that was struggling because its leaders felt they saw market opportunities everywhere – and so they failed to segment or prioritize their opportunities.

The thinking sounds logical enough at the most superficial level: everyone has financial needs and financial plans of some description, so why rule yourself out of certain opportunities?

The trouble is, that's a road to nowhere. If a company's offer is too broad, every day becomes a hard day, because there is no clear means of being purposeful. Just where do you start? This is one of the reasons why, as we've explored elsewhere, clarifying the purpose and the values that attach to your business is so important.

One of the ways we explain this to clients that need some help with the concept is to help them visualize it: we show them a picture of 20 green apples, and just the one red one in the mix, standing out and appealing to its customers against the samey competition. In short, your business needs to be that red apple – it needs to emphasize its difference from those it is up against.

A stand-out offer: four areas of focus

Change your marketing message

How you market your business and its products is likely to change. At its simplest, you are moving your marketing message away from influencing customers through pricing to talking about all the other benefits of your business' products or services. This needs a marketing approach that emphasizes those features of your company's products and services that make them stand out from your competitors. Advertising and promotion may well be through the same channels (social media, print advertising, free product samples, etc.) but the message is different.

Focus on product development

To shift your customer's focus away from the price of your products and services you must place more emphasis on product development. The goods or services your company offers must simply be better made or offer features your competition has yet to integrate into its own offerings to consumers. This may well require constant refinement of your products and services to keep your company ahead of the competition and first in the minds of customers in your market area.

Do your research

Any differentiation strategy must invest time in researching customer needs. Determining what's missing in the market can help with product development and with the marketing message by helping you develop products and services consumers want to buy and by promoting your company as a provider of the best, most-needed products and services in your niche.

Focus on your sales team

All the money you put into product development and advertising will be lost if the sales team can't land more and more business. Sales staff need thorough training in the strengths of your company's products, including what separates them from the competition and any special features that are unique to your business. Attending to the sales is not a one-off but an ongoing commitment to sales training and staff composition. The goal is to find the right mix of staff members and training techniques that produce the best results.

Better is often about service rather than 'features'

In lots of markets, and as with the logistics example we covered above, we have found it is often easiest for small businesses to stand out for their customers through better service.

Of course it's perfectly possible for your product to set you apart too, but does your roll-call of product features really deliver an advantage to customers, and set you apart from the competition? Very often features are, for customers, a list of the obvious or the irrelevant. So how do your product features stack up if you apply a critical eye?

Service, on the other hand, describes an actual, lived relationship – between you and your customer – which makes delivering something **UNIQUELY** useful that much easier to achieve.

Markets are always changing

When looking for your point of difference, it's also important not to confine your thinking because **EVERY** market is constantly being redefined in some way by someone to create spaces and new opportunities. You just need to be bold and become one of those leaders.

In the beauty industry, it might be a males-only grooming offer that creates a niche that wasn't previously there; in the holiday and leisure sector, maybe it's a low-cost airline undercutting the established competition or flying to destinations that others don't. Or perhaps it's a child-free (or, conversely, a family-friendly) offer that will help a hotel business stand out from the competition. Then again, differentiation might be through a clear innovation: something like the children's travel gear range developed by Magmatic in Bristol, whose Trunki suitcases defined a new market where there was nothing similar before.

Really our point is a simple one: opportunities abound. Wherever you look in business there are different variables at work in every market, and new opportunities emerging, and markets being created, by ambitious, confident business owners who aren't afraid of shaking things up and seeing if the demand is there for something new.

Keep the customer satisfied

Many of these new business opportunities, as we've mentioned elsewhere, will spring from the demands of the customers themselves, because what makes a particular product or service attractive to a particular buyer may be something the seller has never fully explored. But the point is you shouldn't be waiting around to stumble onto opportunities like these but be ready to go and grab them by constantly keeping up the dialogue with customers and by pushing forward.

In part this chapter is, then, a plea to shake yourself out of any complacency around delivering for customers, and to treat the opportunity as a real fight for market share. This is something that's particularly pertinent in today's shrinking, globalized world where the opportunity to make high-margin sales based on being in the right place at the right time is vanishing fast.

The nursery with a difference

Ask any parent of pre-schoolers about the challenge of juggling the working week with sending a child to nursery and the opening-hours conundrum will likely come up.

In most nurseries, pick-up times are a fixture for mums and dads and guardians to keep to, and late pick-ups are nearly always discouraged through financial penalties.

For one nursery operator, however, this daily challenge for busy working parents and guardians has been turned into an opportunity and a point of differentiation for the business.

Rather than penalizing latecomers, the nursery has given parents the freedom to be late at short notice periodically. This is billed as 'happy hour' and gives parents and carers an hour's worth of late time per month that is now built into its contracts. The goodwill this new service has created among parents since its introduction, and the distinctiveness of this parent-friendly approach, has transformed the popularity of the nursery. For the first time since its launch it is now running at full capacity with a growing waiting list. The cost of delivering the service was relatively small but the outcome has been extraordinary.

Building on this simple idea, the nursery has been extending into other parent-friendly initiatives, including a 'clean kids' policy that commits, well above and beyond health and safety guidelines, to keeping the nursery environment clean and healthy at all times and to sending all children home at the end of the session in their own clean clothes.

The upshot of these and other initiatives has also been a virtuous circle of success: goodwill from parents, waiting lists for the service, strong interest from would-be employees in working at the nursery and improved finances for investing in improved facilities and future expansion.

All this from the acorn of an idea to reduce some of the pressure on parents when a working day overruns or doesn't go to plan.

Taking those smart next steps

Working out how to differentiate your business offer in the eyes of your customers marks yet another beginning for the business, of course.

In the next chapter we'll start to explore how you can ensure that you build on your particular point of difference in the most strategic way, whether that difference is based primarily around cost leadership (unlikely for many SMEs), some mix of differentiated products or services or has its basis in building smarter relationships with existing customers.

Keep reading!

Three ways to stand out from the crowd and please your customers

Want to make your products and service the only choice for your customers? Here are three ideas:

1. **Be really different.** To differentiate yourself enough, some would say you **REALLY** have to stand out. The goal is to be so clearly set apart from the others in your market that customers really don't need to consider shopping around.

   Many brand strategists say that brand differentiation comes about not by introducing yet another marginal difference but by creating whole new categories or sub-categories that redefine the market in such a way as to make competitors irrelevant or less relevant.

   Put another way, just touting a feature or benefit that offers marginal additional value is not enough. You need to go further.

2. **Business to business companies should think like they sell to consumers.** Your customers are people who want something that will add value to their lives – whether the business is B2C or B2B. Since so much has been written about branding in the B2C market, there is an opportunity for B2B operators to learn certain lessons from B2C and apply them. That's because the process is the same – and the bottom line is to take care of customers.

   B2C branding often focuses on customer value and satisfaction in real detail. Apply that to B2B and see things happen.

3. **Business-to-business customers are human too.**
As a follow-up to Point 2, B2B companies need to remember that they are reaching out to individual people, just like B2C businesses do. Companies are never just dealing with 'the decision-maker' but with 'Jackie the CEO', or 'John the finance director'. In other words, business-to-business is still person-to-person.

This should come out in a branding strategy which could include:

- Use of first-hand testimonials (let your customers become advocates).

- Attending trade shows (face-to-face still counts).

- Listening: listen to customer concerns – and act on them.

- Co-collaboration: to solve any issues customers are facing.

- Becoming a cheerleader: to show just how much your customers' success matters.

Chapter 10

Are you staying out of the killing fields?

Let's begin this chapter with a big question. What happens when a company starts selling just the right things (whether a product or a service) to the right customers in the right way?

It's like magic, that's what – and the whole world starts to look different. This chapter is a chance to explore that magic.

What about the title, then, with its reference to 'killing fields'? What's that about?

Don't worry, it's all part of the same idea: 'stay out of the killing fields' is the title of a session we sometimes run when we are working with boardrooms at Business Doctors. It's one of the tools we have used down the years to explore this idea of selling the right thing to the right customers in the right way – because the flip side of getting this spot on is that you end up in the 'killing fields' as a business. By this we mean that you aren't competing well enough on:

1. Cost (by mainly having a cost focus and going head-to-head with the competition on price).

2. Differentiation (by having a strong focus on your point of differentiation in the marketplace).

3. Having a strong enough niche offer.

So the 'killing fields' idea is just our way of visualizing the particular problems that arise when the business is unfocused: that is, you risk ending up as a commercial also-ran with no specific competitive edge. If you look at these three ways to stand out to your customers as three points of a triangle, any business model that isn't taking the customer offer towards one of those points is by definition located somewhere in the 'killing fields' between them. And that of course is just what we think you should be trying to avoid. Simple, really.

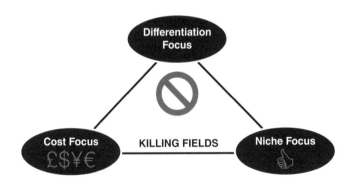

A surprisingly good example here is Tesco. It's been tremendously successful, spending many years as the UK's leading supermarket by revenues and profits. But in recent years it has come under pressure partly because it is being squeezed by the upmarket and downmarket competition. It's under price pressure from the likes of Aldi and Lidl, while its higher-end offer is threatened by Waitrose and Sainsbury's among others. In Tesco's case, its price-competitiveness has not in itself given it a sustainable competitive advantage – and it has languished in the 'killing fields' compared with the competition. (These things are relative, of course! But it's a clear illustration of the point.)

A targeted win

For this chapter, we want to focus on the benefits that flow from getting things right, because everything up to this point has been aimed at getting you and your business plans in the best possible place.

We aren't presuming that your customer offer is anywhere close to perfect, but now is the moment to look at what happens when you do have a really well-targeted customer offer in the marketplace.

First, then, let's remind ourselves of where we've reached.

It goes something like this: to have a successful business, you need a customer offer that is different from and better than the competition **IN THE EYES OF YOUR CUSTOMERS.**

For this to be true, you need to be offering something that aligns with the needs of the best customer groups you've identified – customers who will appreciate the value of your offer because it's a perfect or near-perfect fit with their need.

It's all a world away from the all-too-common marketing approach that sees companies **TRYING ANYTHING** to secure a sale, in the mistaken belief that all that effort will help them prosper.

The harsh reality is that this kind of scattergun approach to business is depressing, exhausting and expensive. The company ends up spending constantly on marketing and sales communications where the proposition is just wrong, and therefore falling on deaf ears.

Of course you won't only be **RIGHT** or **WRONG** in this situation: you could be doing some things right while neglecting other areas of the business that still need to change, but you certainly do need to understand just how important **PRECISE TARGETING** is in today's business world. You just can't try to be all things to all people and expect to succeed.

How has selling changed?

The really big thing here, once you've zeroed in on your customer offer, is that the way goods and services are bought is changing fast. Today's information-rich, socially-driven internet has transformed buying and selling both for individual consumers and for businesses.

Partly this means the old distinctions in marketing and promotional theory, namely between 'push' and 'pull' selling, are changing as well.

As you may well know, in marketing theory a 'push' promotional strategy makes use of a company's sales force and trade-promotion activities to create demand for a product. If it's a consumer product or a commodity item, the producer promotes the product to wholesalers, the wholesalers promote it to retailers, and the retailers promote it to consumers. If the end customer is a business, the strategy looks similar, though perhaps with fewer links in the sales chain, as the company sales team often tries to create demand by interacting with customers or would-be customers directly.

Examples of 'push' tactics might include: trade show promotions to encourage demand; direct selling to customers in showrooms or face-to-face; negotiation with retailers to stock product; packaging design to encourage purchase; and point of sale displays.

A 'pull' selling strategy, on the other hand, is one that uses spending on advertising and consumer promotion to build up demand for a product. If the strategy is successful, customers are motivated to seek out your brand or product or service in an active process. Some call it 'Getting the customer to come to you'. Examples of pull tactics include: advertising and mass media promotion; word-of-mouth referrals; customer relationship management; and sales promotions and discounts.

Many of these tactics are still as used today as ever, of course. So how are things changing?

Like this.

In lots of contexts, it is simply the case that conventional 'push' tactics, especially for B2B sales, are on the way out. It wasn't so long ago that market information was hard to come by for businesses and individual customers looking at a potential purchase, and aggressive sales tactics worked in many different contexts. Would-be customers needing a product or service often found it hard to find what they needed in lots of places or to build up a detailed picture from independent sources about the relative benefits of Option A versus Option B, say. Added to this, perhaps neither Option A nor B was really quite right, and another option entirely was actually what was needed – but finding that service or product was too challenging for a time-pressed business owner.

In today's world, this kind of situation must still crop up sometimes, of course, but the visibility of products and of services has been and is being transformed by the internet and by online search, as is the availability of third-party opinions or useful evidence on goods or services, particularly with the recent rapid rise of social media and online social networks.

It's also possible to buy from geographically remote businesses more easily than ever, opening up genuine global competition in some markets where not so long ago the customer was obliged to choose from a smaller pool of options closer to home.

With all this information so easily accessed, and references and referrals readily available online too, the sale has, not surprisingly, been transformed.

What was once almost the norm in B2B selling and in certain types of B2C selling – a pushy salesperson with an internal financial target to hit and a buy-now agenda in every customer meeting – is being consigned to history.

What's replacing it is a different approach to marketing and sales that puts the customer and would-be customer first, second and third. Today's salespeople are consulting carefully to find the right fit and are quite happy to give away lots of good advice and market knowledge for free in an effort to build a customer relationship.

It might sound like hard work, but once the right fit has been found between a supplier and a customer it can, as we said at the start, be the start of something wonderful.

CASE STUDY 1: The right kind of telemarketer

Here's an example that nicely illustrates the power of a well-matched service to a company in need, and handily also serves to show how customer relationships are evolving.

One regular Business Doctors client is an office supplies and services business in the South West of England with a growing roster of business clients – and an appetite for growth.

The business is owner-managed and turns over several million pounds. It is led by an energetic entrepreneur who could see when he came to us that the company needed to secure new customers more effectively to maintain its growth trajectory.

He had identified telephone-based marketing as an effective sales tool for his services, and was happy to plough a significant investment into this strategy. But the first company he outsourced the task to failed to deliver, having been given free rein to line up 'warm' sales appointments for the owner to attend.

What happened next? Nothing. For several weeks no appointments were booked, and with little else to go on the owner-manager decided to get out of the relationship as quickly as possible.

The problem was that the telemarketing approach he had plumped for, as well as not delivering in terms of meetings, had also not been a good fit in the first place.

For good practical and emotional reasons what he needed was a transparent telemarketing effort that he and others in the business could plug into and help to direct and develop in the right direction – an approach a world away from the appointment-making service he had tried and seen fail.

Armed with this detailed, highly specific brief, we were able to go out to the market and find a company local to him that delivered a service exactly matching this need. In other words, it's a service that means he can sit down and listen to recorded or live telemarketing calls and then suggest any changes that are needed, to ensure the appointments being made aren't 'forced' but are genuine warm leads.

What's amazing when you have this perfect fit between customer need and delivered service is that price becomes secondary – and even close to irrelevant in some contexts.

The business is now paying a top-end rate for a service that is truly delivering, both in absolute sales terms and because it has enabled the feedback loop that the company wanted and could see it needed in order to carry the business forward.

Putting a price on a super-service

Just how pricing works when a product or service that's being delivered is **EXACTLY RIGHT** for an individual customer or a business is worth exploring further.

The point to make first is that, if you can really deliver for any of your customers, it will put the relationship on an incredibly strong footing. It's likely you will be a preferred supplier and you will be recommended and promoted to others enthusiastically by your happy customer. Most of us are shocked to get something that's just perfect, even when we are paying for it, so when you get things right the rewards and the enthusiasm are likely to be off the scale.

When it comes to pricing, you are then well placed to adopt a value-based pricing model when you are delivering in spades for any customer. If what they are buying is delivering great value to them they really will be happy to pay handsomely for that.

What's more, if you can adopt an approach that helps you to create the magic once, even with one customer, you should be well placed to do it again. How did you ensure you delivered so perfectly, after all? Your analysis of the market opportunity with the customer was likely spot on, reflecting the precision of your wider research into your business opportunity.

This puts you in a strong position relative to any competition. Most companies shy away from value-based pricing, because they're afraid of the process and end up rushing to solve other problems facing the business that seem less forbidding. Yet, even though there's work involved, value-based pricing provides real data that automatically pushes the business towards a profit-generating price. Simply put, if done correctly, this approach to customer need and to pricing will quickly help you generate your best-ever margins.

Value-based pricing also describes determining a more accurate price for a product or service because, by exploring the customer and the competition, you better understand the advantages of your offered product – which is precisely where marketing should focus – and where it is still falling down and needs to be altered.

So the up-front work and the ongoing analysis is about much more than pricing – it's absolutely tied up with finding that sweet spot that will have the customers wanting more and paying for something valuable.

Taking on a customer's perspective will also help you discover what your would-be customers are really looking for from you. Products and features will then be driven by customer demand, which raises perceived value, leading effortlessly to a higher price.

A different level of customer service

So how do you deliver like this for customers? Customer data to deliver a perfect customer offer, and priced at the value being delivered, is something you can collect through detailed market research backed up by customer interactions of one sort or another: perhaps surveys or interviews. Indeed, the responses we've seen to simply bringing customers into the discussion, and the value that's being derived by them, have been extraordinarily positive and appreciated.

This attention to customer opinions and wants will improve your service levels, too – which often marks the difference between a one-time customer and a loyal customer that develops a bond with the company and always comes back for more.

Are there any downsides?

Well, clearly the effort we've described here takes time and it takes resources. In short, you'll need the finances in place to see it through to the point where it starts to deliver.

This is not a quick win with a simple return-on-investment calculation and a nice margin. But if there is no shortcut to be had, there is definitely no shortage of opportunity. Even in a sector or market that's seemingly loaded with staunch competition there will be plenty of chances to stand out on your own terms to particular customers – and, having delivered, to name your price. Get this right, remember, and the benefits will flow, with more profit, better and more competitive products, and a customer-oriented marketing and development approach that can sustain the business for the long term.

CASE STUDY 2: The eco-tourism business

An eco-tourism company we worked with made some specific decisions in its market planning after we sat down with them. This was a South African boat-charter business, competing in a market with lots of fishing charter operators in the local area plus some party boats too.

To differentiate its offer, the company decided to offer sightseeing or special event charters, and not to allow alcohol on board the boat – or fishing rods. It was a decision that turned away from a big slice of the market – but it also gave the company a niche to develop and expand. And very quickly that's what happened. It expanded its market in a way that other charter operators with a different offer could not easily compete against, and doubled its business within 18 months.

The basis of that success was how well targeted the charter business was: it primarily reached out to those would-be customers who just wanted to feel good – spending a day out on the water, relaxing and being waited on. It also targeted people who had visitors coming from out of town, or even overseas, because it offered a solution to the problem: 'What will we do while our guests are here? How can we entertain them or show them the area?'

The business had a primary market that was national or international – tourists who visit from all over the world – and a secondary market that was local: that is, those who have a special event to celebrate, a company meeting or retreat to plan, or guests visiting from out of town.

It proved more than enough of a differentiator in an otherwise crowded market, where most of the other businesses were going head-to-head against each other using aggressive sales tactics, and frequently being beaten down on price.

Understand your niche: the B2B dynamic

For any business selling to other businesses there are lots of variables to consider when eyeing your perfect customers.

Businesses buy products or services for three reasons only: to increase revenue, to maintain the status quo, or to decrease expenses. If you can deliver against one or more of these needs, you may have found a target market. To get to that point, here are some questions you may end up asking:

- What industries are worth targeting and why?
- What size of company, in employee terms, works best?
- What annual sales volume and location is most appropriate?
- How stable are the companies we want to target?
- How do our would-be customers purchase? Seasonally? Locally? Only in volume? Who makes the decisions?

Once you've done this kind of research in a detailed way, you should know with some degree of accuracy how big a pond you are fishing. Is the number of potential customers high enough to sustain the business you want to create? What proportion of those potentials will you need to convert to customers – and is that realistic? If it turns out to be too niche, you might need to revisit some of your presumptions and come up with a revised plan.

But the underlying point is clear: there's a market, and a target market, for every business.

Understanding your particular sale

We've already talked about how the philosophy of selling is changing. The next chapter will look in detail at handling those precious customer relationships – and at how to think like a customer at all times.

Before we move on, though, let's reflect more on that question of the philosophy of the sale in a context where you are aiming to be the perfect supplier business.

1. **Have an intense focus on the prosperity of your customers.** For many, that requires nothing less than a U-turn when it comes to the psychology of the sale. No longer do you measure your own success first. Instead, you measure success by how well your customers are doing with your help.

   It also means you're not focused on selling a specific product or service, but instead are focused on how your company can help the customer succeed in all the ways that are important to that customer. By tapping the many resources you have at your disposal to help customers meet their business goals and priorities, you are adding value every step of the way.

To do this effectively, as we've suggested, you'll have to devote large amounts of quality time and energy – much more than you do today – to learning about your customers' businesses in great detail. What are your customers' goals? Which financial measures are they most keen on? How does your customer create market value and what are the key factors that differentiate his product or service from those of his competitors? It's only once you have done this that you can look for ways to help the customer – in the short, medium and long term. The greatest opportunities will naturally lie in the medium and long term, where you and your customer can work together to change the nature of the game in your customer's industry based on value you can help provide.

2. **Use capabilities and tools that you've never used before to understand how your customers do business – and how you can help them improve that business.** Sales are no longer just for the sales force: you need to muster the help of people in many parts of your company to do it. Staff from many different departments, including the legal, finance, R&D, marketing and manufacturing, will need to become intimately familiar with your customer. You'll be compiling large amounts of information about your customer, both facts and impressions, in useful databases that are shared and used to determine the best approach for helping your customer win.

This will surely demand that you build new social networks, both within your organization and between your organization and the customer. Information will have to flow in both directions, and there will be a need for frequent formal and informal interaction among people serving different functions within your company and between your company and the customer's.

3. **Make it your business to know not only your customers but also your customers' customers.** It is no longer enough simply to satisfy your customer's demands. You also have to know what motivates those next in line down the supply chain – what their problems and attitudes are and what decision-making processes they use. In order to tailor your solutions to your customer's market, you'll simply have to know about the bigger picture.

4. **Understand that the execution of this new approach will require longer cycle times to produce an order and generate revenue.** Patience, consistency and a determination on your part to build a high degree of trust with your customers will be key. This is imperative because in this new relationship the two-way information exchange is far deeper than that you have relied on in the past. But once it gets going, the cycle time can be very fast, because you will have established trust and credibility.

5. **Re-engineer the company's recognition and reward system to ensure that the organization as a whole is fostering the behaviours that will make the new sales approach effective.** In this context, quarterly sales targets and the like cannot be the only basis for rewarding the sales force. What's

more, other members of the sales team from various functional areas must be recognized and rewarded proportionately for their contributions. That's only fair, too.

In the next chapter, we'll look in detail at the customer and the customer relationship, and drill down into the behaviours and tactics and thinking that will really pay off. In the meantime, with customers and customer service on the brain, here's a checklist to ponder.

Seven ways to serve your customers

1. **Be quick about it.** In a world where everything is fast, and so much is time-based, speed can still give you the competitive advantage. So when dealing with customers, fast service will add value, show you care and secure trust.

2. **Communicate with positivity and purpose.** Take responsibility for your communication – the purpose of your communication is the response you get. Speak the customer's language and cut out jargon. Make written communications short, specific and simple. Talk benefits rather than features.

3. **Keep it personal.** You build a business one customer at a time. People like to deal with people they like, know and trust. Always be courteous and be polite. Use the customer's name regularly in conversation. Accommodate customers' special requests wherever possible. Get to know your customers, all of them. These are simple keys to building trust, respect and loyalty.

4. **Keep those customers.** Customers usually go else-where because the people they deal with are indifferent to their needs. The cost of attracting a new customer is many times the cost of keeping one. So keep them happy however you can.

5. **Turn complaints into opportunities.** Complaints are opportunities, and problems are wake-up calls to let you know something is wrong. Customers who com-plain are valuable because they want to remain custom-ers and are simply telling you how to achieve this.

6. **Exceed expectations.** How often are your customers wowed? The world is full of mediocrity. It takes vision and commitment to make or do something better. So establish clear expectations and then exceed them.

7. **Deliver, deliver, deliver.** Competence wins every time. Training is not a cost, it's an investment. Standardize systems to ensure consistency. Think through processes and methods to pre-empt all situations. Aim for success and plan for failure.

Part Four

MAKE IT HAPPEN!

A company that has an offer that's ready to take to the world is only part of the way to guaranteeing its success. Much else remains to be done, and this final part of the book explores some of the remaining detail that matters, from how to have excellent customer conversations, to finding and keeping the very best people, to the need to develop and track metrics that really do measure the important stuff.

Chapter 11

How to have great customer conversations

Not so long ago marketing was often about shouting the loudest, and selling to customers meant aggressively trying to convince would-be buyers you had what they needed.

Today's marketing agenda is changing fast – and already looks profoundly different.

As Chapter 10 explored (and as we've touched on elsewhere too), nowadays you need to work hard for the benefit of your customers – and then keep on working hard to deliver just what they want and need. (If it's a B2B context, that means you need to keep demonstrably adding value to the customer's business.)

It's an approach that's far removed from old-school selling – and the distinction is only going to get more pronounced as the best companies take marketing, and the sale, in this new direction.

Community before commerce

For companies that are committed to their customers, today's sales and marketing approach rests on having good conversations and building trust. And more and more, that also means putting community before commerce. What does that mean exactly? It means being helpful – truly, deeply helpful – and then trusting to commercial karma that being supportive and open will repay itself in new relationships and a broad base of trust that will lead to new business.

And what form does being helpful take? Perhaps the main development is the new primacy of **content marketing**.

Plenty of prominent marketing thinkers say that content marketing should be viewed as the leading form of marketing today. They want businesses – once and for all – to stop interrupting people with irrelevant messages and start providing them with information that is genuinely useful – either professionally or personally. Successful marketing has become all about sharing valuable information, or 'content', with buyers and would-be buyers.

For many companies, this requires nothing less than a radical shift in thinking. And it probably means wresting access to services, and all of the detail of what the business does, away from that old-school sales team in order to deliver your stories and expertise and insights in new ways for various audiences.

Here, to get us started, is one 'before and after' take on how things are changing:

Old-style marketing:

- A fancy website filled with sales puff.
- Costly press advertisements.
- Pushy sales people.

- A glossy brochure.
- Badgering the trade press to write about you.

Today's content-led marketing:

- An engaging digital footprint (including your website) that's easily found by potential clients.
- A dynamic social media presence that makes targeted connections.
- Great word-of-mouth recommendations.
- Heaps of valuable content for use in lots of contexts.
- Trust that builds as you keep on providing proof of your word.

Both marketing approaches – the 'old' and the 'new' – aspire to attract attention. Both try to make your message memorable and to sell products and services. But it's the shift of focus that makes the new marketing approach a better proposition for business owners. Getting to grips with how your clients think, understanding their needs, and being clear about the problems you can solve for them is what will give your business an advantage.

And remember: starting is not difficult. It just means listening, asking questions, and then doing even more listening. Take the spotlight off your proposition – and shine it on your clients. What problems are they facing? How can you help them?

As we've said elsewhere, you can use this knowledge to create the kind of services your clients want, and build your content around it. Today's marketing never underestimates the intelligence of the customer. So if you've done your homework and your offer is right, there will be no need for those desperation 'sign up now!' calls, because **YOUR CLIENTS WILL COME TO YOU**.

Is old-style marketing finished?

Before we move on, one question that's natural to ask is whether this shift in approach signals the death of traditional marketing. In fact, we don't really think it's dead – merely altered. What we are describing here is how 'old' methods are being approached in a different way.

Business development experts talk about building-in would-be customers, the motivation to buy by leading with the valuable stuff and only selling when the time is right. In this context, well researched and valuable content demonstrates quite brilliantly that you understand your buyer's world – better than any brochure, e-shot or clever marketing device ever could. And if you can show the customer that you really do understand the critical success factors facing that business **WELL BEFORE** trying to sell, that's often enough. The customer might just find you interesting enough to actively want to meet you.

In other words, traditional marketing techniques are still there and will always have a place. But the best way to employ them is as a follow-up proposition lined up behind all those content-related efforts.

This content-first approach can take many forms. For example, it might mean sending your customers a business book or article that gives a new perspective on an issue you know they are facing, then following up with a phone call. Or it might see you emailing something useful or entertaining along with a short note. Or you might look to advertise an informative event in just the right place.

Whatever the marketing tactics, what's needed across the board is the right mindset: never shouting, pressurizing or trying to manipulate, but instead understanding, respecting, helping, educating or entertaining the would-be buyer.

As the marketing gurus have it: the best marketing is about understanding those you want to reach – and then creating something valuable, interesting or entertaining that's targeted right at them.

Engaging with the customer

OK, so you've got someone's attention, helped them out with some useful advice, and now have a meeting lined up.

What's called for now is a bit of sensitivity and plenty of listening: the days of selling as an act of manipulation – of prospecting, contacting, pitching, persuading and convincing – are over.

Selling no longer describes something that you do **TO** a prospective customer. The idea is not to push through any objections, move your agenda forward and close the deal.

Selling like that creates antagonism, and it's a product of an impatient mindset, when what you need to build mutually beneficial long-term relationships is the opposite: you need **PATIENCE**.

Consider the ultimate impatient sales approach: the cold call. On its own it's essentially ineffective – and especially in a B2B context. A call might work after a 'trigger event', like someone viewing the company website, but making contact should really only be the start of something long term and helpful. That means the 'sales process' or 'sales funnel' no longer consists of the steps that the seller must take to make the sale. Instead, it should aim to track the smaller decisions that would-be buyers must make before they can make that final decision to buy.

Here's two scenarios to consider to get you thinking along the right lines:

- Someone visits your website and registers with the site. It then makes sense to contact that customer to see if you can answer any questions the person might have. It's an offer to do something for that person rather than to try to convert them into a customer.

- Think about what it is to be a customer who is working through the internal politics of deciding budget priorities. You'll just irritate people if you start calling trying to drum up financial support for your offering. You're more likely to make the sale if you work at figuring out what the customer needs to make a decision.

None of this is meant to imply that you should sit back and just wait for customers to buy. There is usually some action that's required – but only action that is respectful of the customer's natural buying process.

Meetings

It's time to shift our attention now to the meeting, and the first thing to say is this: a meeting with a would-be buyer, which might lead to a sale down the line, is clearly not the only way for products and services to be sold. However, it's still true that this kind of 'push' marketing and sales approach performs a crucial role in most businesses, and is absolutely fundamental to the average small business that is selling to other businesses. What's more, the world of 'pull' marketing is changing fast, too, with social media having transformed the nature of many consumer sales, making them more consultative and less transactional.

When it comes to sitting down face-to-face with a would-be buyer, this is of course potentially a massive area to explore. While we won't be getting in too deep here, there is also ground that we can usefully cover.

The first obvious point to make is that preparation is crucial for any meeting, whether it's an initial getting-to-know-each-other chat or something with more of an agenda. Further down the line the relationship with an established customer will take on the character of a partnership – and any meetings will feel very different.

For those early meetings with would-be customers, every company representative needs to have thought about possible outcomes and objectives connected to and arising from any forthcoming conversation. And, if it's a first or second meeting, they partly need to be clear in their own minds about the extent to which the customer is free to drive the agenda and dictate the pace.

If a first meeting has been set up on the back of plenty of helpfulness and goodwill and the sharing of useful content to reach this point, carrying on in that vein is fundamental. But meetings need some energy and purpose to them too, and there are many ways to approach them even if old-school pushiness is off the table. (After all, your time is valuable and meetings without purpose are potentially damaging to your bottom line!)

You need to listen!

Whatever has gone before, any early meeting with a would-be buyer is a chance to listen. But how to listen exactly? There are plenty of influencing styles that sales people have used over the years. Even if some don't really fit with today's no-pressure approach, it's worth summarizing them.

- **NEGOTIATION.** As an influencing style, negotiation relies on offers of trades, bargains, compromises and concessions in order to reach agreement. When negotiating, positive and negative trades are used to influence the other party. To be able to use negotiating as an influencing style the original proposal or idea must have areas where compromises can be made without jeopardizing the overall success, and those areas that are negotiable must be important to the other party.

- **VISION.** The vision influencing style paints the 'big picture' of what the future will be like. It relies on people sharing a common goal or a common objective which is described in broad terms and which is easily understood. It generates enthusiasm and energy by appealing to values, aspirations and concepts. It inspires commitment and excitement often by using colourful language and pictures and building emotion.

- **LOGIC.** This style depends on using the power of logic and reason to influence. Proposals are presented in a logical and structured way, where elements are considered in detail objectively and lead to final conclusions. Facts are used to support arguments and intangible factors are relegated or dismissed.

- **PEOPLE ORIENTATION.** People orientation is characterized by a desire to work with others and to influence by creating an environment where ideas are listened to and suggestions built on and developed, generating commitment by involvement and shared ownership. It works in a climate of encouragement, praise, support and recognition. When using this style, arguments are considered from the perspective of those involved and the effect on them. Implementation questions are also addressed pragmatically.

- **ASSOCIATION.** As an influencing style, association uses support from influential groups or expert knowledge. The support can be nurtured or can be won by responding to political sensitivity by actively aligning ideas to those where support will be easily won. To be successful, individuals must be sensitive to the real sources of support and where association will be of benefit. It is a style that is often used informally to win acceptance.

One or other of these approaches may well sit comfortably with a particular company representative, as well as fitting with the nature of a particular discussion – and with the personality of the would-be buyer. So it's worth ensuring your company representative understands some of these influencing styles, and can potentially make use of them in some form when appropriate.

Preparation and structure

Many sales experts like to approach a business or sales meeting as a step-by-step process. While that might sound too structured and formulaic in the context of our preference for customer-led interactions, it is also true that nearly all meetings – particularly follow-up meetings – will need an agenda (not necessarily written down) and proceed in at least a semi-structured way.

How to approach these meetings? Here are some useful pointers to help out. We've written them as if you are the one doing the preparation, rather than another representative of the business.

Planning and preparation: Generally, the larger the prospect organization, the more research needs to be done first in order to ask sensible questions and to present the company's products or services in the right light.

- Ensure you are fluent with your own proposition products/services – and especially those features, advantages and benefits relevant to the would-be customer.
- Think through the main or unique perceived benefit that your proposition would deliver to the customer.
- Explore the current supply arrangements for the product or service and assess what that supplier's reaction is likely to be if this flow of business is threatened.
- Understand what other competitors are able and likely to offer, and which ones are being considered if any.
- Identify as many of the prospect organization's decision-makers and influencers as you can, and assess as far as you can what their needs, motives and relationships are.

- Try to get a feel for the organizational politics.

- What are the prospect's organizational decision-making process and financial parameters? (For example, budgets, year-end date.)

- What are your prospect's strategic issues, aims, priorities and problems? If you can't discover these pre-meeting, what are they generally for the market sector in which the prospect operates?

- Prepare your opening statements and any possible business or product presentation.

- Prepare your presentation in the format in which you are to give it (for example, leaflets, presentation slides) plus all materials, samples, hand-outs, brochures. Always have spares –allow for more than the planned numbers as extra people often appear at the last minute.

- Prepare a checklist of questions or headings that will ensure you gather all the information you need from the meeting.

Openings: How to get things off on the right foot.

- Smile – be professional, and take confidence from the fact that you are well prepared.

- Introduce yourself – first and last name, what your job is and the company you represent, plus what the company does (ensure this is orientated to appeal to the prospect's strategic issues).

- Check anticipated timings, including the duration of the meeting.

- Ask if it's OK to start by asking a few questions or whether an overview of the company would be useful.

- Set the scene – explain the purpose of your visit and orientate it around the would-be buyer and his or her needs. Lead the conversation by making sure you are the one asking the questions!

Questioning: This goes to the heart of most meetings.

- The main purpose of questioning is to confirm or discover the strongest or unique perceived organizational benefit for the would-be customer from using the product or service.
- Questioning must also discover how best to develop the business with the organization – how they decide, when, people and procedures involved, competitor pressures, etc.
- Good empathic questioning builds relationships, trust and rapport – nobody wants to buy anything from someone who's only interested in their own products or company.
- You will have prepared a list of questions or headings – use it now.
- Use open questions to gather information – who, what, why, where, when, how and which. To do this, you should kick off with broad background questions which demonstrate your interest in their business. (But don't instantly go for the jugular by asking what the budget is! Imagine how you would feel walking into M&S and being stopped at the door by the manager and being asked how much you had in your wallet before being allowed to look around the store.)
- Use 'can you tell me about how' if you are with a senior contact – generally the more senior the contact, the bigger the open questions you can ask.

- Use 'why?' to find out reasons and motives that often lie beneath the initial answers given.

- Listen carefully and empathically, maintaining good eye-contact. Show that you understand – especially that you understand what is meant and felt, not just what is said, particularly when you probe motives and personal points.

- Interpret and reflect back and confirm you have understood what is being explained.

- Use closed questions to qualify and confirm your interpretation – a closed question is one that can be answered with a yes or no.

- When you've asked a question, it's time to SHUT UP and listen!

- Your would-be customer should be doing at least 80% of the talking.

- Do not jump onto an opportunity and start explaining how you can solve the problem until you have asked all your questions and gathered all the information you need. (Never be seen to 'jump' onto any issue.)

- All the time, work to find out the strategic issues affected or implicated by the products/services in question – these are where the ultimate decision-making and buying motives lie.

- If, during the questioning, you think of a new important question to ask, note it down or you'll forget it.

Your turn to talk: (If the customer wants to listen.) When you have exhausted the questions, and when you feel that you have enough information to talk with a relevance and brevity about how your proposition can address specific needs, it is time to get permission to talk.

To unlock this, start by summarizing the areas and needs that are relevant to the proposition with a very natural lead-in: 'So, just to check my understanding of what you have said . . .'. Once you get back a positive response you can ask if the would-be customer would like to hear how you can possibly help. Once you get a 'yes' it's definitely your turn to talk. Ideally at this stage you should deliver a verbal summary, not a standard presentation! Try to focus on a central proposition, which should be the unique perceived benefit that the would-be customer gains from your proposition.

Here's what you need to cover off:

- During the questioning phase you will have refined the understanding (and ideally gained agreement) as to what this is. Your summary should focus on 'matching' the specific benefits of the product with the needs of the would-be customer so that the would-be customer is entirely satisfied that the proposition fits.

- You need an excellent understanding of the many different organizational benefits for the customer, and to be able to back up the points made.

- The summary must demonstrate that the product or service meets the would-be customer's needs, priorities, constraints and motives.

- All business summaries must be well structured, clear and concise, professionally delivered and demonstrate integrity.

- The summary must avoid simply talking about technical features from the seller's point of view, without linking the features clearly to organizational context and benefit for the would-be customer.

- Summaries must always meet the expectations of the listener in terms of the level of information and relevance to the would-be customer's own situation. Remember those influencing styles!

- The summary must include relevant evidence of success, references from similar sectors and applications, facts and figures – all backing up the central proposition.

- Business decision-makers buy when they become satisfied that the decision will either make them money, or save them money or time; they also need to be certain that the new product or service will be sustainable and reliable, so the summary must convince here too.

- While the summary must always focus on the main perceived benefit, it is important to show that all the other incidental requirements and constraints are met.

- Summaries should use the language and style of the audience. For example, technical people need technical evidence; sales and marketing people like to see flair and competitive advantage accruing for their own sales organization; managing directors and finance directors want clear, concise benefits related to costs, profits and operating efficiency.

- Keep control of the summary, but do so in a relaxed way; if you don't know the answer to a question, say you'll find out and get back with an answer later, and make sure you do.

- Never, ever, knock the competition.

- Only use props and hand-outs and demonstrations if relevant and helpful.

- During the summary seek feedback, confirmation and agreement as to the relevance of what you are saying, but don't be put off if people stay quiet.
- Invite questions.
- Relax and be friendly, letting personality and natural enthusiasm shine through. People buy from people who love and have faith in their products and companies.

Negotiating and other moves: (Because it's not always plain sailing.)

- Successful modern selling now demands more initial understanding ahead of a first meeting, so the need to overcome objections is not prominent these days.
- But objections do arise, and they can often be handled constructively. This is the key.
- If objections arise, first you should acknowledge the objection.
- Then qualify each one by reflecting back to the person who raised it, to establish the precise nature of the objection – 'why do you say that?' is usually a good start.
- It may be necessary to probe deeper to get to the real issue, by asking why to a series of answers. That's because some objections result from misunderstandings, and some are used to veil other misgivings that you need to expose.
- Lots of objections are simply a request for more information, so definitely avoid responding by trying to re-emphasize the benefit – simply ask and probe instead.
- Avoid altogether the use of the word 'but' – it's confrontational.

- Avoid old-style techniques to tackle objections, such as re-phrasing a question that's been put to you and tackling that. Also avoid trying to isolate the objection and then overcome it.

- It is important to flush out all of the objections, but it's also best to work with the would-be customer to understand what lies beneath each objection in order to work with the customer to shape the proposition so that it fits with what's required.

- Avoid head-to-head arguments – even if you win them you'll destroy the relationship and you'll go no further.

- At this point it may be appropriate to keep notes and show that you're doing it. It will help you cover all the ground you need to but no more.

- Respond to any early buying signals by asking why the question is important, and then by answering as helpfully as possible.

The close: (You won't always need this but you must be prepared.) First point here: a 'no' is better than an unconcluded meeting. It gives you the opportunity to deal with a reason for a 'no' and simply move on. Worse than a 'no' is a disguised 'no', usually presented as a stalling 'not sure'. This is nearly always a brush-off when the buyer prefers not to give you the real reason for saying no.

With that, let's get back to the close:

- In effective meetings, even if a structure has been followed, there should be no need for a formal close.

- In many cases, if you conduct the meeting properly, the would-be customer will close the deal. This should be the aim for you as it's civilized, respectful, and implies and requires a high level of business professionalism.

- The manner in which a meeting is concluded depends on the style of the decision-maker – watch out for the signs: no-nonsense high-achievers are likely to decide very quickly and may be a little irritated if you leave matters hanging after they've indicated they're happy; cautious technical people will want every detail covered and may need time to think, so don't push them, but do stay in touch and make sure they have all the information they need; very friendly types may actually say yes before they're ready, in which case you need to ensure that everything is suitably covered so nothing can rebound later.

There should be plenty there that's useful. Before we close the chapter, we've just time for some further thoughts on the customer-first model of business engagement we've set out here, with content marketing to the fore, a customer-centric approach throughout, and the right kind of face-to-face meetings.

Do some business models make face-to-face unnecessary?

A question that arises naturally from our extended exploration of the face-to-face meeting is whether there are business models that can circumvent face-to-face entirely.

One approach that's gained ground in recent years that appears, at first glance, to do away with that need for content marketing as described, and for a consultative approach in general, is the '**freemium**' or tiered approach to selling software.

Freemium's proposition is different in that it promises to build most of its trust through demonstration rather than by content marketing and face-to-face helpfulness. (It also works well with software because the cost of production – of replication – is negligible.) It may also sound appealing to plenty of business owners concerned about the challenge of how and what to sell, since the model looks so different: offer content or a stripped-down version of your service for free, avoid paying for sales reps, conventional marketing or advertising, and instantly win tens of thousands of customers, some of whom will convert to a paid version of the product. Simple!

Or maybe not. The trouble with that simplified description is that freemium doesn't automatically work like that. The formula might look simple but it still needs a clear-sighted approach to the cost and mechanics attached to securing a paying customer if it's to deliver on that ideal.

Just like any business product or service, a freemium software offer needs to get quite a few things right in order to stand a chance:

1. **Pick a market that actually exists.** That is, the market must already have a set of customers that are paying money to solve a definite problem.

2. **There must be a clear gap in this market.** This could be a customer segment that is under-served or a product or service not delivered in an ideal way or some other failing that your offer overcomes.

3. **Freemium also needs to be targeted at a niche that's actually chargeable.** The proposition must

help people or companies make money – and especially in a market where spending habits are already proven.

4. **The model needs to offer just the right level of value with the free service.** The free service must ensure that *anyone* can get *some* value without having to pay, and that those that upgrade to the paid version get something exceptional.

There's more that we could drill down into here, but the basic point to make is this: mastering this particular business model teaches us all over again about the importance of getting a sale process right, because fundamentally it still requires an acute understanding of how to deliver usefulness, build trust and then turn that trust into paying customers and long-term relationships. There should be lots of data being generated by the process, too, yet only a few content creators are so far using that data wisely and are able to answer satisfactorily those fundamental questions about the cost of delivering the service versus the ability to generate revenues from paying customers.

If the freemium strategy amounts to a simple call to action – 'Here's a free sample. Now sign up for the paid version to get even more!' – then it's doomed to fail. To convert would-be customers to paying customers, they still need to be guided down a specific, helpfulness-oriented path, in a particular non-pressurizing way, for the sale to land. And that's not easy.

The sales funnel just got narrower

One lesson to take away from all of these ideas around marketing and sales is that getting your particular niche or proposition just right is still crucial, whatever your likeliest route to a committed paying customer.

Perhaps, then, that familiar sales-funnel visual we can all conjure up now needs to be laid to rest. A funnel suggests trying to reach out to lots of potential customers before a filtering process gets underway to find those that fit best. In fact, all that we've explored in this chapter and in Chapter 10 emphasizes how the need to differentiate and carve out a particular space that's extremely attractive to only particular customers is the way to take things, with all the follow-up marketing and sales work being similarly targeted and focused on supporting individual customer needs.

Really that funnel looks more like a cone or an arrow now, doesn't it? The logic is that we want to get in just the right would-be customers to fill up that cone, and then develop those relationships first through dedicated helpfulness and, eventually, by working with them as well-supported partner-customers.

Partly, too, this journey is likely to be about cleansing, because not all of your existing customers will fit with this vision. If some customers were acquired in the past through price competition or on adversarial terms then those customer relationships will need to be reset where possible or else some customers will be gradually let go. This is a transition phase that's hard to avoid – and it has to be handled with care because in your brave new world of stronger customer relationships not all customers will be created equal: some will still be stronger or more profitable or a better fit than others. You'll keep working towards a particular ideal, but it's in the nature of thing that you'll never quite get there. The point is to aspire and to keep trying and moving forward in just the right way.

Recap: stop 'selling' and start building relationships

Old-style sales and marketing techniques are counterproductive, but how do selling behaviours change if you change your sales thinking?

- **The traditional sale:** Always deliver a strong sales pitch.
- **The new sale:** Stop the sales pitch and start a conversation.

When contacting someone, start with a conversational phrase that focuses on a specific problem that your product or service solves. One example of an opening phrase might be, 'I'm just calling to see if you'd be open to exploring some ideas related to cutting your risks around systems failure?'

- **The traditional sale:** The main objective is always to close the sale.
- **The new sale:** The goal is always to discover whether you and your potential client are a good fit.

If you don't try to 'close the sale' you will soon discover that you don't have to take responsibility for moving the sales process forward. If you simply focus your conversation on problems that you can help potential clients solve then you soon find potential clients drawing you into their buying process.

- **The traditional sale:** Rejection is an everyday part of selling.
- **The new sale:** Sales pressure is the only cause of rejection. In fact, rejection should never happen.

Rejection happens if something you said triggered a defensive reaction from a potential customer. To cut out rejection just give up the hidden agenda of hoping to make a sale. Once you do, everything you say and do will stem from being there to help potential customers, and the conversations can take on a different character.

- **The traditional sale:** Keep chasing every potential client until you get a yes or a no.
- **The new sale:** Never chase a potential client as that creates sales pressure.

'Chasing' potential customers is rooted in the old-style selling logic that equated stopping chasing with giving up. This isn't true. Instead, tell a would-be customer that you would like to avoid anything that resembles a chasing game by scheduling a time for your next chat.

- **The traditional sale:** When a would-be customer offers objections, counter them.
- **The new sale:** When a potential client offers objections, look to find the truth behind those objections.

Never focus on 'overcoming objections'. Such tactics fail to explore or understand the truth behind what a potential customer is saying. Instead, uncover the truth by gently exploring whatever it is that customers are objecting to. You should be able to politely get them to reveal the truth of their situation.

- **The traditional sale:** If a potential client challenges the value of your product or service, you must defend yourself and explain the value.

- **The new sale:** Never defend yourself or what you have to offer as that's a form of sales pressure.

When someone says: 'Why should I choose you over your competition?' they are showing that they don't want to be sold to. The best response is to say that you aren't going to try to convince them of anything because that would only create sales pressure. Ultimately you want potential customers to feel that they can choose you without feeling they have been sold to.

Chapter 12

Pressing the reset button

Once you've got the strategy, you can now work out who you need on the team to make it happen.

And it's not just in the boardroom that skills and motivation matter, of course, but right across the company.

So this chapter – and we hope you agree it's a crucial chapter – is about the company and its people. As your business vision and all your plans come to together, implementation means finding and holding on to the right people with the right talents, and then getting the best from them. In many ways, too, some of what we'll be exploring is an extension of the ground we started to cover in Chapter 3, which looked at creating the right company values and culture. We've left it until now to develop these ideas further around the people challenge only because the logic of the book – of how to develop your business in the right way – has demanded that we cover so much other ground first.

What are you (less) good at?

When it comes to thinking about the company and its people, the place to start is naturally right at the top.

What a leader may be really good at, and also not so good at, are important elements to understand. The most successful entrepreneurs are astute and analytical enough to recognize their strengths and weaknesses in order to pull in the right resources to help a business take root and grow. Someone like Richard Branson, with his Virgin empire, has always been recognized as being good at this – at understanding what he can and can't do, and focusing his effort on those areas where he adds real value, while bringing in outside talent to assume other crucial positions.

And there are plenty of other examples out there from current and recent business history: think of James Dyson, with his engineering genius but reported dislike of the boardroom, or Steve Jobs at Apple, which as a business has always been recognized as willing to invest in finding the very best in order to stay ahead.

At the same time, we know this isn't an easy area for many business leaders to explore. Entrepreneurs are usually optimistic types, which can make it very hard for some to recognize that they are not good at certain things. It takes a lot of soul-searching for someone to understand their own core skills and strengths. After that, it should be a question of finding the smartest people out there to complement those strengths. But it's also easy, of course, to be attracted to, and so want to bring in, those who are most like you – rather than finding those with talents you don't have.

Good at presenting? Great. What about your management skills, then? And what about all the detail of running the business? Does getting analytical with the data to unlock your business understanding tend to excite you – or just bore you silly? Is motivating and inspiring more your style?

Our simple point is that there is no sense is getting hung up on trying to be **THE** leader, with a finger in every pie. A leader who's a control freak and can't let go of the reins in any context never helped any business – in fact, it is often the single biggest blockage to serious business growth.

Understand where you fall short

Sometimes it's obvious what a particular leader is good at – but not always. There may be areas where a leader clearly excels, but others where someone is comfortable and feels competent yet may not really have all the skills or understanding or empathy that's needed. Equally there will be those areas where an owner-manager or founder knows they are weak and is happy to reach out for support.

So it's that grey area in the middle that can make this a challenge, and one that may well need outside support to tackle.

In our work as Business Doctors we sometimes think we can see where a leader we are working with needs some help – but the challenge then can be to get the leader to see what we are seeing. Mostly, in fact, we don't like to rely on our instinct in these matters, with so much as stake. It's often better all round to try to be analytical about strengths and weaknesses, because you'll end up with something 'objective' that is easier for everyone to accept and act upon.

How do you get analytical? Well, there are plenty of psychometric profiling tools out there that can help, and we are enthusiastic users ourselves. But the toolkit also extends well beyond the simplest psychometric profiling into more detailed 360 reviews and the like – and we use these too.

Such reviews are professional feedback tools designed to help anyone from a CEO to a store clerk develop and hone their professional skills. While a standard job review is about the job an employee is doing, a 360 review is focused on the person. In a 360, you get the combined perspective of several peers about the team work, communication, leadership and management skills of any individual – it's personal and powerful, and can apply to the founder of the business just perfectly if that's who needs it.

Putting the business first

What we are advocating here, in relation to people, is a business-first approach. You need the right person at the top, who understands his or her role, and that needs to continue through the business – with the right people performing the right functions for the right business reasons.

It sounds obvious, doesn't it? But a great many businesses are **NOT** in fact built around the needs of the business but **AROUND THE PEOPLE** the business is being run by. That's because the leaders of the business have avoided taking the necessary tough calls and allowed the talent management and the recruitment strategy – and therefore the business – to drift.

A blank sheet can shock

If you think that description sounds a bit extreme, consider tackling this task: pretend you just bought the company as it looks today. Putting aside any relationships you have, get out that metaphorical blank sheet and decide what job roles the company **REALLY** needs in order to thrive. As part of this process, what are the lines of connection between those roles that the business ideally needs?

If you take this exercise seriously, we'll be amazed if what you create is anything like your real set-up, which will have been built in all likelihood around on-the-hoof recruitment decisions, ill-defined job roles, changing personal relationships, longstanding loyalties (perhaps even family ties) and more.

Hard to do? Here's one we made earlier

In fact, we'd be amazed if you produced anything meaningful on your first go. Most company boards that have tried to carry out that exercise with us down the years have found it, as described, almost impossible to complete. Why? Because the existing relationships they have in the business, and how that defines the current shape of the business, make it incredibly hard to look beyond the present arrangement with any objectivity.

We've found the best way through this common impasse is to come at it with something ready-made. If a blank-sheet approach to the challenge is a bridge too far, how about fitting a conventional boardroom arrangement onto the business?

It's amazing how consistently the leaders of companies of a given size — usually those with a few million of turnover, a few dozen staff — will quickly see the benefit of a boardroom and company structure that just sticks to the main lines and keeps things logical and simple:

- **A managing director** to take the lead on strategy and on managing a motivated team of people to deliver it.
- **A sales and marketing/business development director** with a top-line focus on the best possible margins.
- **An operations director** delivering the right product or service, on time, in full.
- **A finance director** to stay on top of the financial side of things, naturally.

Once it's described like this, with a tier of management below the board and reporting right in to the relevant director, many leaders will be able – all of a sudden – to see only too well the benefit of this approach over the spider's web of relationships and roles they are working with currently. Often it's nothing short of a revelation.

MD – or shareholder?

This radical depersonalizing of the business and its future needs can throw up another dynamic, too. By getting a leader to think dispassionately about the business we are also tacitly (or sometimes explicitly) asking them to assume the role of shareholder rather than employee. It's all part of the necessary journey of letting go that any business owner contemplating a future sale will soon have to travel.

By starting to think like a shareholder, some can start to think the unthinkable about that top slot, too: what if the best managing director for the business isn't the current owner-manager but someone else entirely? What if a sideways or downwards move is what's needed for the founder or MD, while others step up?

Too radical? We don't think so – and we hope you can instinctively see why. A director of a business is meant to be acting in the **BEST INTERESTS OF THE BUSINESS**. That's the function and purpose of a board, after all. A director has to act properly in that role and put the business first, or he or she is not really a director at all.

Director – or manager?

With company hierarchies front of mind, it's worth exploring this idea some more. If the boardroom directors of a business should have one set of priorities, and the shareholders another, in many companies confusion reigns since playing fast and loose with job titles is a way that some try to keep the interest and enthusiasm of those in important day-to-day middle management roles.

Is yours one of those businesses? You know the kind: somewhere where anyone who's anyone in the business is called a 'director' when in fact most are managers of a small team, feeding performance through to the board from time to time, and nothing more.

The problem with this approach – or one problem, at least – is that the mentality of a manager with a steady, senior job but no boardroom responsibilities is usually very different to someone sitting on the board who is focused on keeping the company solvent, profitable and on the right side of the law.

Managers, indeed, are often protectionist in their behaviours and want to maintain the status quo, when what might be needed is something much more radical.

What we are talking about here, of course, is the **INDIVIDUAL ACCOUNTABILITIES** of those in a business. And we are saying that being clear about roles and responsibilities right across a business matters a great deal to its success. If the current set-up is messy and confused, we know this isn't something that can be changed overnight, but it's still important to start driving things in the right direction as quickly as possible, usually as part of a wider people-engagement exercise that can be applied right across the business.

How to find the right business talent

1. **Look under some rocks.** Finding the right people requires effort. You don't want to be overwhelmed with candidates who all look the same, but you do want enough candidates to be selective. Try to reach out beyond your usual sources to find skilled candidates you might have missed.

2. **Hire juniors on potential, seniors on specifics.** This one is logical. The further down you are hiring in the company, the more you are looking for potential rather than specific experience. When it comes to senior hires, you'll need more specific skills, experience and expertise.

3. **Get excited by new talent and new ideas.** Some leaders worry about hiring someone too senior who might threaten their existing team. New teammates

should be an OK fit within a culture, but also help to push the existing team to make it better. So always embrace the opportunity to hire strong talent.

4. **Consider the opportunity cost.** When you choose one person you are rejecting everyone else. Use that choice wisely and someone will stand out.

Engaging with staff

So far we have considered a few big questions you need to ask yourself when it comes to the handling of some of the people in the business, and to finding the right newcomers. But that's only part of the picture.

The next step – and an even bigger piece in the puzzle – is to start reaching out and asking questions of those in the business already, and then being prepared to act on the answers you get. Since the business has to come first, and the profile of the people within it must be built around its needs, engaging with and talking to everyone in order to get the best from them is fundamental.

To get the ball rolling in this area, we often conduct staff engagement sessions, putting mixed groups of staff together, getting them off their job for a few hours and into a different environment.

A day like this starts with a short presentation outlining the core values, core purpose and visionary goal of the business and emphasizing that any plans being aired are by their nature provisional and will need all the staff to pull together to deliver them.

It's a session that's designed to engage and to motivate, and it's built around asking those taking part for input and ideas to help the company reach whatever goals have been set. Four questions or challenges usually help to frame the session:

- **Structure and communications:** How should we be organized as a business?
- **Productivity:** How can we become more efficient and productive, and hence more profitable?
- **Growth:** How should we improve our sales performance and business development?
- **Recognition:** How can we recognize and reward your invaluable input?

As you can see, it's all big-picture stuff – giving the staff a sense of the vision for the company, but in an engaged, two-way process rather than in the form of a broadcast.

The aspiration is that it should be a great motivator for those who attend, but the session is unmistakably also the first step towards giving **OWNERSHIP** of a business to the staff and hence making everyone **ACCOUNTABLE**. If there is a consensus about how to do things better and who should do particular things, you very soon reach a point where you can roll out ideas as fully formed plans – and with measurements attached. It's a powerful mix.

Is there a flipside here? Yes there is. You must understand that not everyone will be energized and motivated by a session like this. You cannot do much about that in some cases, though maybe you can in others. Motivation comes from within: all a business can do is provide the right environment to motivate its people and then hope that it works in most cases.

Where significant change is needed, an engaged team will feel they are equally responsible for promoting change and the actual change process will be much easier. In fact, even those being released when the reset button is pressed will at least understand why it is happening and realize that this organization is not right for their particular skills and aspirations.

The four 'Rs'

A strategy day like this is a failure unless a proportion of the staff buy into it fully. Where it works – and it usually will on some level, so long as you follow through properly – it means you can press the 'reset' button on the business and its people and start to plan for the future.

What does pressing 'reset' mean? It means starting afresh with a vision for how the business should be staffed, and what the lines of accountability should look like.

There are four people-related 'Rs' that attach to this part of the process. They are:

- **Retain:** the good staff who support the business model need to be retained and valued.
- **Retrain:** where there may be good people, but there is a deficit in their knowledge or experience, retraining is needed.
- **Recruit:** where there is a gap, recruiting the right person or persons to fill it is crucial.

- **Release:** when necessary companies have to be prepared to let those people go who don't fit with the business model or ethics.

Easily summarized, but this stuff can take time of course. This is where you can set the clock ticking, however, and get a process of change fully underway.

The fifth 'R'

The fifth 'R' that fits with this process is **recognition**.

Everyone wants recognition; everyone wants a heartfelt 'thank you'. In fact, don't forget that often that's all that's needed. 'R' might also be said to stand for **reward**, and people like to be rewarded too. But try not to overlook what a great motivator proper recognition is. A late-night email to someone that acknowledges all that they have done on a high-profile project, or an impromptu private one-to-one to say thank you properly: this stuff matters. Often it matters that much more than that end-of-month bonus that's taken two months to be signed-off and added to payroll. It's a point worth remembering as you begin to embark on potentially such a sweeping change process.

Simple change, big impact

If that's the theory, how does this work in practice? Every journey is different, but here's a quick one that's worth sharing as it might motivate you to get started!

Some years ago we worked with a construction company whose staff revealed, over the course of an engagement day, that they were embarrassed by the mess in the owner's office when clients visited. They also felt that the company required stronger branding – a sign outside the office, signage on vans, branded overalls, to name just three of their ideas. The owner wasn't well liked by many staff – he was seen as aloof and high-handed – but he reflected on the suggestions at length and eventually decided to adopt them across the board. In the next 12 months company turnover increased by £1m (from £4m to £5m) and profits jumped by nearly 20%. Follow-up surveys found that most of that jump was traceable back to that moment when the staff were listened to and really trusted to make the business better.

What difference could it make to your business, do you think?

Three ideas for employee engagement

Getting employees engaged requires the right approach:

1. **Your questions need some focus.** If you are asking employees for ideas, give the request some focus. Don't put: 'Send us your ideas to help grow our business'. Do put: 'Please send your ideas for how we can make our packaging wording easier to understand'. Or: 'Submit your ideas for how we can eliminate injuries on site for the duration of the build'.

2. **Make sure you follow up.** Nothing is more demotivating for employees who want to share ideas than to have those ideas ignored or filed away. If you collect

ideas in a suggestion box you then need to act on that. If you don't, it says that the employees' ideas aren't valued and perhaps suggests that the request wasn't serious in the first place. The sharing of ideas shuts down very quickly if a business doesn't follow through, so consider establishing a committee or a plan to review ideas on a weekly or monthly basis.

3. **Share and celebrate.** Some believe that unless an organization is willing to 'pay' for ideas, employees won't be interested in sharing. So scour your company history for success stories that started with a single idea from an employee or a group. Try to share the story of what inspired the idea, and how it changed as it was developed.

Four ways to support new starters

1. **Tell them all you can about the business.** There is always pressure to get new employees 'up to speed' and commercially effective. But first new employees should get to hear first-hand what the business is 'all about' and learn its core values. Concentrate on this first, and only then train newcomers about the everyday.

2. **Make sure you understand how they can deliver for you.** Don't be afraid to look closely at the return on investment that a new starter can deliver. Invest in employees early so they become profit centres for the business as soon as possible.

3. **Listen and learn.** Every new starter will bring new expertise and experiences to the company, and you should embrace the change that they may bring. Ask that

they speak up when they see something that was done differently, and possibly better, at a previous employer. There may even be grounds for coaching them on how to share insights with you and your team without being seen as hyper-critical. For example, new ideas are more easily accepted if they're framed as open-ended suggestions rather than criticism.

4. **Help them to understand the power of engagement.** If new starters and existing staff alike are involved across the board in the process of change it gives all staff ownership of what needs to happen. You end up with a motivated, joined-up group of individuals all striving for a shared vision that they collectively believe in and want to make happen.

Chapter 13

What gets measured gets done

Our final chapter is all about measuring what matters to help you make informed decisions. There's no question that this matters hugely – and, if you are ready to start following through in other ways, by applying some of the ideas explored elsewhere, this is a crucial final piece in the puzzle that helps to get the business on track.

But we have an important question for you to get things going: does business measurement and analytics sound like something to avoid? Does it sound dull to you – or a hassle? We really hope not, even if we understand that getting out there and creating new market propositions, making new relationships and winning new business is, for many entrepreneurs, a whole lot more exciting than collecting and analyzing important data to try to understand things that bit better.

But if you've made it this far with the book, we hope you are now some way down the track in terms of being ready and willing to explore the change your business needs – and that means more measurement.

Have no fear!

Many energetic entrepreneurs don't warm to this stuff. We know that from first-hand experience and from exploring it with many clients. What's more, with any business that is struggling at all there's a strong tendency by many to give up on any notion of being strategic and analytical in favour of cash-chasing. Does that sound familiar? For plenty it will.

Not being remotely strategic may be illogical but it's certainly a very human response. If a business is operating in a short-term cycle, chasing cash from one month to the next in a never-ending game of cash flow cat-and-mouse, how much attention is likely to go into metrics and measurements – particularly if that analysis is only likely to shine a light on a company's many frailties? For many, head-in-the-sand seems preferable.

All we have to say here is this: the fear factor may be under-standable but it's not acceptable to anyone serious about embarking on business change.

Another thing that holds back plenty of business owners in this situation may not be fear of the hard numbers in them-selves but of the hard conversations and relationship pres-sures those numbers are likely to trigger. As soon as you start to explore areas of 'failure' or poor performance it opens up the prospect of conflict, doesn't it? Shining a light into the dark corners of a business is never going to be comfortable for any management team.

But none of these dynamics provides a good reason not to tackle things head-on. Accountability and transparency and honesty are the bedrocks of any successful business and its boardroom – and your business is no different.

Beyond dispute

The upside of gathering meaningful data for analysis is that numbers can tell the story in an unembellished way. If you are tracking the right metrics to understand a business, it's hard to argue with the numbers that are collected.

We aren't saying there won't be conflict – it will be likely for many – but as a basis for an accurate discussion, relevant data is a whole lot better than a room of half-informed opinions. It really is time to jump in.

Metrics that matter

First steps

What should you be looking for? What data should you be looking to collect?

There are usually a few dynamics and contexts to consider here. Typically there's the top-level information that will give you a picture of the company or divisional performance; next up, there might be the metrics that will help to track the performance of certain teams or projects; and, as you start to drill down, there will be metrics that help certain key individuals to measure their performance, track progress – and be rewarded when they deliver.

But this is a long-term play; you shouldn't try to do everything at once. Mostly you can start small, working out what particular bite-sized pieces of information will be of most use in selected contexts as you get the process underway. And remember: this may not merely be useful but can be transformative even from early on – because for many senior individuals in a business, the ability to track and measure and demonstrate performance will come as a relief and open up new and exciting ways of working.

The basics

Every company has to track its financial performance. The ebb and flow of money from the company accounts of even a relatively small company will usually involve thousands of transactions in a typical year, and with tax obligations in the mix every company has to maintain and keep a detailed log of the financial fundamentals.

Yet, with so much data at the fingertips, it's still surprising how many business owners fail to pay proper attention to those basics of **REVENUES VERSUS COSTS**. Instead of rigorously scrutinizing what's coming into the business, and setting that against the outgoings for each revenue line, it's still surprisingly common for many company directors to wait for the accountants to tackle the annual company accounts well after the event and to sign them off for filing with barely a glance. It's out-of-date information, goes one argument, so why bother?

That way lies trouble, needless to say. Up-to-date, properly maintained management accounts are a fabulously useful tool to every business – so start to look carefully at them, and pull out what's most useful as regularly as possible, if you aren't already.

Regularly? For simplicity let's say **MONTHLY**. What are your key revenue streams and **WHAT IS COMING IN AND GOING OUT** each and every month? Forecasting is crucial here, too. Are those numbers up or down on expectations – and how did you set those expectations in the first place? Prior-year performance or some other point of comparison?

It's simple stuff, we know, but every business has to get a firm grasp on the fundamentals – and in a meaningful way, with the data examined to generate sensible areas for scrutiny.

Consider, for a moment, a lift company with three core revenue streams – new-build business, modification and repair work and service contracts. How much is each part of the business bringing in each month? And what costs attach to those sales – again, with each revenue stream treated separately? The analysis gives a company its **SALES/REVENUE** figures and its **GROSS PROFITS**, broken down by revenue type. Once other overheads are accurately added into the mix you then also get a **NET PROFIT** figure for each revenue line, too.

We hope you view this all as simplicity itself. It really is. But if you aren't thinking along these lines you should know that you aren't alone: many company directors we have supported down the years weren't tracking their monthly revenues, gross profits and net profits from month to month when we first sat down with them, and they certainly weren't projecting from those numbers with forecasts for the months and quarters that lay ahead.

Cash flow

Cash flow matters to every business – though some have a bigger cash flow gap to plug than others, perhaps because of the nature of the industry they are in (e.g. manufacturing) or for certain historical reasons, like a big customer moving a key contract onto worse payment terms.

Whatever the particular dynamic here, the object must be to take control of your cash flow understanding as quickly as possible. What are your outgoings from month to month and how and why do they vary? What money typically flows in, and what is the story behind it? This is granular work, but it needs doing: it matters. You need a cash flow model that is intelligible to give you back some financial control that may have been missing. It might reveal that your credit control is weak, for example, which is something that is relatively easily remedied and could have a positive effect on your situation by giving you the breathing space you need to start planning and stop cash-chasing.

Profit and loss

In our experience, if you can **ACCURATELY** allocate your costs in your business you will learn a great deal very quickly.

While it's an easy goal to set, it's actually often harder to deliver than you might think. Revenues flowing in are simple enough to capture, but how were those sales secured exactly? Here's a few elements that might be on your checklist to explore, with the aim of putting a value you can trust on the cost of each sale:

1. How many enquiries were there set against actual sales?
2. What was the conversion rate of sales-related meetings against sales?
3. How much time elapsed between an enquiry and the issuing of an invoice?

4. What was the average order value?

5. Is there any correlation between order value and the sales process and personnel that applied?

6. What kind of dynamics applied for each of your identified revenue streams? Similar sales process and metrics or distinctly different in each case?

7. How can we capture the different routes to a sale in relation to sales and marketing activities?

8. Which marketing activities are most successful and most measurable? Which activities are hard to measure in success terms – and why? Which activities are most successful – and why? Which activities are least successful – and why?

We can bring this to life by talking about our own experiences. At Business Doctors about 60% of customer leads come from the programme of free seminars that every Business Doctor runs. Typically we get 30 business people along to a seminar, of which five on average will ultimately sign up and work with us.

Viewed at this top level it's a simple formula – far simpler than for many businesses. The seminars are our front end, raising interest in our offer to company directors that translates into a flow of opportunities and business. But beyond that we can drill down and start to look at all the elements and variables and costs (time costs and administration costs and marketing costs and sundry other overheads) that go into each sale. Beyond that, there is a tier of work to be done looking at the profile and value of particular customers. What is each customer worth? And what is the story behind that value to the business, and behind the value the business is adding to make the relationship and the investment worthwhile for the customer?

All of this kind of analysis is customer-focused, and useful on those terms, but our point is that much of it is also feeding the profit and loss account and an understanding of the profit margins and business volumes that attach to a particular revenue stream. And the more you can measure, the more you can start to understand what counts and what works in terms of customer value and the customer mix.

The customer mix is an idea worth saying something more about here too. A business might find it is too reliant on a handful of clients and needs a broader spread of customers spending slightly less. It might also find that analysis reveals that certain customers share certain attributes and can usefully be categorized and treated in similar ways. So you might have category-A customers, category-B customers and category-C customers accounting for nearly all of your business, plus some others that don't fit the formula so straightforwardly. The customer grouping will take many forms, but financial measures will play a part in this categorization, perhaps alongside other common attributes.

Once you start to pull back a bit from this kind of work you'll find that some of the now-available financials are invaluable in terms of insight – and can point the way ahead. For example, knowing the average order value of particular customers, the gross profit per customer type and the net profit per customer is just the kind of data that will make a difference when trying to set meaningful performance targets and financial goals in the years ahead.

Big business, little list: Tesco and its KPIs

We hope it's clear by now that every company, large and small, needs to be tracking its most important financials, both as a means of forecasting and planning and as a yardstick to measure progress.

Tesco is one of the UK's biggest businesses, but it tracks just three top-level financial 'key performance indicators' ('KPIs' for short: today's favoured way of describing such measures):

- **Growth in underlying profit before tax:** this measures, in percentage terms, the growth in the underlying financial performance of the business, stripping out accounting adjustments and one-off costs to arrive at a meaningful measure of financial progress.

- **Return on capital employed:** this is a relative profit measurement, given as a percentage, that measures the return the business is generating from its gross assets.

- **Growth in underlying diluted earnings per share:** this is the amount of underlying profit in the business, adjusted for the number of shares in issue.

Next to this, it also tracks and publishes about 25 other KPIs that measure activity and progress, with some, like its annual capital expenditure as a percentage of sales, helping to reveal the shifting strategic aims of the business in a changing economic environment.

The point we are making here is that the big-picture metrics are crucial for giving that tangible, black-and-white insight into a company's progress (or lack thereof). The strategic detail may be found elsewhere, in all those niche metrics, but to understand whether the effort you are putting in is working, in overall terms, you want to stick to simple, understandable and fair measures of financial progress.

The waste recycling business

A producer of waste disposal furnaces that we worked with transformed itself through measurement and monitoring. The company's main failing had been its persistent failure to undertake professional, advanced job costing. Instead, it had tended to quote for jobs based on what it had charged for similar work in the past, without sufficient scrutiny to know whether its rates made sense.

On our advice a financial controller was recruited with job-costing experience and the impact was instantaneous. Early analysis revealed that nearly all of the company's work was more time-intensive than the company had believed, and once this was factored in properly, using real measures, average profit margins climbed fourfold.

The company's customers, for their part, were buying a high-value service that was extremely valuable to them and they weren't all that price-sensitive: almost without exception they were prepared to pay more for the service when new contracts were negotiated, while the percentage of customer wins against sales meetings actually increased. Customers responded to the professionalism and transparency of the newly-costed projects, with every element documented, and didn't baulk at the price.

So why had the previous way of working arisen in the first place? Purely and simply because the company was being run

237

without enough commercial focus by a management team mainly consisting of engineers by background. Those in the business proudly understood the technology and the innovation they were delivering – and so they delivered a technical sale without enough attention to the finance side of the sale. Where were they falling short? One example lies in how they typically might have estimated two hours for working on the personalized elements of a contract, when even cursory hours-tracking and analysis showed they usually spent a minimum of ten hours delivering that bespoke service.

Getting personal: how do you measure soft skills?

Top-line financials matter, then. But, at the other end of the spectrum, so does individual performance if a business is to succeed top to bottom. And when you reach the point of starting to look at the best measures of personal performance to make a difference, a different question arises. How do you square this focus on measurement with an emphasis on developing the personal skills a senior manager needs to succeed?

The answer is to approach the challenge with some lateral thinking. Since you can't really measure the soft skills themselves in a satisfactory way, the best way to measure personal qualities and personal performance is by looking at related indicators. If a company has a customer retention rate of 90%, for example, it probably shows that soft skills are strong within a customer service team, and by extension that the head of the team is delivering. It's not a perfect solution but, properly applied, it will often deliver what you need to know.

Structure, vision and measurement

There's something else worth drawing out here, which is that measurement is partly about accountability across a business – at the individual, departmental and boardroom level. As such, this work goes hand in hand with some of the work we outlined in the previous chapter around boardroom and company structures.

Remember that common boardroom and company structure that we identified as so often working for companies of a particular size?

- A managing director
- A sales/marketing/business development director
- An operations director
- A finance director.

Well, if you have the right sort of company structure in place – and perhaps this one fits the bill – that's also something that you can easily link the right measurements to. A handful of key metrics – four to six? – that are each 'owned' by a particular boardroom member whose job it is to see that their measure is heading firmly in the right direction, is a powerful recipe for business success. With this sort of structure in place, performance excellence can cascade through a business, driven by the accountability of individuals and divisions to deliver on a particular set of targets.

This work on measurement and company structure is also something that links strongly to the idea of developing a vision for the company, as we explored in Chapter 5.

We said in Chapter 5 that developing a vision that your company starts to live by will carry it a long way. Well, metrics are one of the crucial tools at your disposal to live by that vision.

If the goal is to grow the company from £1m to £7m turnover within five years, as in our Chapter 5 example, tracking and living by the right set of performance metrics is a crucial tool in your push to get there. Remember all those long-term company-vision questions we set out by way of example:

- How many staff will it have, and with what skills?
- How much space will it need?
- Where might it need offices?
- What technologies will it be using?
- What partners will it have?
- What leadership team will it need in place to run effectively?

Well, before you get to that point – which is meant to be five years away, after all – there are plenty of other data-related questions to try to ask and answer first about the company's journey, to ensure it is driven and measured in a virtuous cycle of striving and informed best practice. And it's only by having a vision in the first place that you can establish your growth plans on sound foundations underpinned by real metrics.

A sales team without targets

A packaging business we started working with had a small sales team where the individuals were paid commission on any sales achieved (as a flat percentage of revenue) but none had a sales target to strive towards, with each sales person managing his or her own diary and documenting sales achieved month to month.

There was no framework for improvement and the sales achieved weren't ever set in the context of the wider improvements and changes to the business, which were many.

For any company that generates a slice of its business from the consultative sale, informed target-setting is a must-have. Fair and transparent activity targets and revenue targets and profit targets should all be in the mix, with the sales team feeling connected to and appreciated by the other parts of the business that their crucial roles serve.

It's something we brought in immediately by initiating a consultative and inclusive process where the sales team got to set much of the agenda and define the reasoning behind their newly-minted targets. Further down the line a sensible restructuring of the department also improved accountability while raising the status of the team within the company.

The end result? Sales climbed by a fifth in the first year, profits by a quarter – and no one left the team either.

Change is everywhere: learning from online

All our talk about the need for businesses to start measuring their most important activities could be taken to suggest that

241

performance measurement is a generally neglected area for business today. In fact, we should emphasize that's far from being the case. In some contexts, in fact, more is being measured within businesses than ever before. However, what is true is that that this measurement-push is being driven substantially by online business, which makes measurement easy for committed businesses, and is still often being neglected by some old-school real-world businesses that may have set up online but aren't yet at the ecommerce cutting edge.

What traditional businesses can learn from the online pure-plays and the best of the multichannel operators is the mentality of embracing constant metrics-driven improvement. Highly measurable activity has changed the rules in certain contexts, whether its hotel bookings websites switching pay-per-click advertising on and off from hour to hour based on their available inventory, or a retailer like John Lewis measuring and comparing its sales activity hour by hour rather than week by week or month by month and making changes online whenever it wants. It's an exciting world – and on some level it needs to be understood and embraced.

A shift in vision and a culture change

We hope the message has come across loud and clear: implementing measurement and accountability at every level of the business is one of the things that will help to cement the vision you create for your company, as well as helping to define the company's culture.

Holistic, lasting change is only possible in a business if the leaders involved are prepared to embrace the kind of root-and-branch transformation that holds the key to unlocking the potential that's latent in many of the UK's small businesses.

With *Breaking Big* we have tried to give you the tools to go on that journey on your own terms, at your own pace – but with personal accountability and a joined-up approach that takes everyone within the business on the same journey at the heart of the vision we hope you now look to establish.

As we said at the start, this is a vision and approach that needs to be *lived* every day by those in the business if the new culture and new ways of working are to take hold.

It's an enormous challenge, but it should be fantastically exciting and rewarding too: get it right and you will see the business fly, and an optimism and energy take hold right across the business. The kind of positive performance culture that lies at the heart of this approach won't be for everyone in the business, but most will quickly embrace it and thrive on it.

It's the people that really matter of course. Ultimately it is the people in the business that will deliver this story, so above all else work hard at ensuring they are engaged and motivated, and feeling purposeful and rewarded at all times. Get it right and their happiness and enthusiasm will carry the company wherever it goes, and your customers will be carried along too, taking delight in engaging with and buying from you. None of this will happen overnight, of course – set your sights on a transformation over two to four years – but if you and those around you keep going and retain a drive and purpose at all times it will definitely happen.

That's it. It really is time to go out and achieve your vision. How do you want to start?

Praise for Business Doctors

'Business Doctors have given us a new systematic approach to running our business in a way that gives us the logic and clarity to finally move forwards.'
Greg Spencer, Managing Director, vet-tech.co.uk

'Business Doctors were able to look into our business with a fresh approach and a keen eye. Their rational approach to tough decisions has been a revelation to our business. Working with Business Doctors has also given us great confidence in the service we provide and where we're heading. Highly recommended.'
Bernard McCabe, Dreamscape Solutions Ltd

'Working with Business Doctors has allowed me to put together a full sales plan for the next 5 years and has given me a true focus and goal of where I want to take my business.'
Jason Rogers, Director, Pinnacle Chauffeur Services

'I honestly don't know how I'd have coped without the help of Business Doctors. It's been a great experience – I've managed to grow my business and become closer to my staff.

Business Doctors have helped me understand and motivated me no end. Best decision I've made in business.'
Pete Gibbs, Owner and Director, Gibbsco Ltd

'After considering taking on a business coach for our family business, Business Doctors were our obvious choice due to their ability to understand our individual challenges and take the time to get to know us. In order to work with someone to make your business prosper and grow you need to have confidence in your coach and this is exactly where we stood. Working with Business Doctors, we are now starting to see results that we didn't think would be possible.'
Jan Lord, Guide Bridge MOT & Service Centre

'Business Doctors started to work with me last year to assist me in developing a coherent strategy for the profitable growth of the business. It should be acknowledged that Business Doctor's contribution to the development of the business has been both real and tangible, even in the short time in which they have been involved with us. Their all-round business skills and financial experience, and pragmatic but systematic approach to working with me and others in the business, have been in evidence often.

I feel personally re-energized, focused and enthusiastic about the future of this business and would have no hesitation in recommending Business Doctors to help an SME owner/ manager to develop their business and achieve their desired outcomes for the future.'
Nikki Walker, Chief Executive, West Midlands Home-based Care (UK) limited

'Business Doctors gave us exactly what we needed – external focus and challenges so that we wrestled with the right issues and good advice in areas such as sales and marketing. They were easy to work with, attentive to the issues we faced as a business, flexible and helped us move from talking about it to doing something about it.'

Mark Withers, OD & Strategic HR Consultant, Group Facilitator, Speaker and Author; Chair, CIPD Thames Valley

'The Business Doctor's approach is both professional and understanding. They have the ability to guide those in business who are lost, and provide solutions that work. Business Doctors are well respected within the local business community and I am pleased to have them on board as a personal contact.'

Paul Butler, Business Development Director, The Black and White Agency

'Business Doctors are technically astute and communicate very effectively, and were enthusiastic from day one. They enabled us to look at our business from a totally different perspective. We have identified specific areas for growth and also where we can improve on what we already do.'

Colin George, Advice For Business

'Business Doctors have given me the confidence to try new ideas, step out of the day-to-day routine and get excited about the future instead of being despondent.'

Stacey Dunne, Owner, Hartpury Saddlery